RESET

www.penguin.co.uk

ALSO BY DAN HEATH

Upstream: The Quest to Solve Problems Before They Happen

ALSO BY CHIP AND DAN HEATH

Made to Stick: Why Some Ideas Survive and Others Die

Switch: How to Change Things When Change Is Hard

Decisive: How to Make Better Choices in Life and Work

The Power of Moments: Why Certain Experiences
Have Extraordinary Impact

RESET

How to Change What's Not Working

Dan Heath

torva

TRANSWORLD PUBLISHERS
Penguin Random House, One Embassy Gardens,
8 Viaduct Gardens, London SW11 7BW
www.penguin.co.uk

Transworld is part of the Penguin Random House group of companies
whose addresses can be found at global.penguinrandomhouse.com

Penguin
Random House
UK

First published in Great Britain in 2025 by Torva
an imprint of Transworld Publishers

Copyright © Dan Heath 2025

A CIP catalogue record for this book
is available from the British Library.

ISBN
9781911709725

Interior design by Ruth Lee-Mui
Printed and bound in India by Manipal Technologies Limited

The authorized representative in the EEA is Penguin Random House Ireland,
Morrison Chambers, 32 Nassau Street, Dublin D02 YH68.

To Amanda, Josephine, and Julia, my three loves

Contents

Contents

1.

There was a red phone in the receiving area at Northwestern Memorial Hospital. It rang constantly. Usually, it was a nurse or staffer calling to inquire about a package: *Where is it? I ordered it days ago!*

In response, the person fielding the call would go hunting for the person's package, which could be challenging, since the receiving area looked like a hoarder's attic. A photo from the era captures the vibe:

In 2016, it took an average of three days for packages to get from the receiving area to their destination in the hospital. Three days.

Just to linger on the absurdity: A nurse might order some vials of medicine, and FedEx might fly that medicine across the country in one day, and then getting that medicine from the receiving dock to, say, the third floor of the same building would take another three days.

It was actually worse than that. Because there was a considerable amount of *variation* in the delays. If the delivery time had been predictable—three days to wait, every time—then the hospital staffers could have adapted. Built in a buffer time. But the wait was sometimes one day, sometimes five. It was plan-proof. It was maddening.

The consequences of the delays were severe. Sometimes medicines requiring refrigeration would spoil, right in the box. Sometimes clinicians and staff, fearing packages were lost, would reorder the same items—often using expedited shipping—which spiked expenses. Sometimes people would try to bypass the receiving area by having packages delivered directly to department floors, making it impossible to maintain an accurate inventory system.

No one liked the way the system worked. But it had been dysfunctional for so long, the dysfunction had come to seem like the natural state of affairs. *Of course it takes three days to get a package delivered. It has always taken three days.*

The receiving area team was stuck.

This is a book about getting unstuck. You'll learn how to reset your work and start making meaningful progress again.

Feeling stuck is dispiriting. The failure to improve and thrive can seep into your self-image. "I didn't make progress" can easily slip into "I'm not *capable* of making progress."

That defeatist mentality prevailed in the Northwestern Memorial Hospital receiving area. "We were just the pariahs of the hospital," said Paul Suett, who joined in 2016 to serve as the hospital's supply chain performance manager. He'd been hired to restore sanity to the receiving area.

"My role was to show them that there's another way. . . . There is a way to succeed," he said.

To unlock progress, Suett knew he needed to get his team to rethink the way they worked. As Paul Batalden, a health care expert, once said: "Every system is perfectly designed to get the results it gets." Meaning that once you change your aspiration—when you set your sights on *different results*—the system you have is wrong, by definition. Because the system is designed, intentionally or not, to yield the results you got yesterday.

Suett had inherited a system designed to deliver packages in three days. And to him—given his background in performance improvement—some of the refinements needed were immediately obvious.

But for change to happen, it wasn't enough for the improvements to be obvious to him. They had to be obvious to his team members, and they had to *want* to make the changes.

He asked them, "If I can show you how to simplify your work—and make it easier on you—then will you come along on the journey with me?" They agreed to listen.

He started by asking them about their own complaints: What was getting in the way of their ability to do good, quick work? Several of them brought up the carts that they used to deliver packages—the carts' wheels frequently jammed up. It was annoying and slowed them down.

Suett agreed, instantly, to buy new carts. The costs were trivial relative to the cost of the department. And it was a signal to them: I really am listening.

He challenged the department to reach a new goal: delivering packages within one day of arrival. That's what their "customers"—the people they served in the hospital—would want from them, he argued, and that's what they needed to provide.

He invited his team to help him diagnose the "waste" in the system. Waste (a topic we'll explore in chapter 7) is defined as any activity that doesn't add value for the customer. Suett's team came to realize that every time they picked up the red phone, it was waste. Every time. Because their internal customers *didn't want to have to call to check on a package*! So even if the call was handled promptly and politely, it was still waste. The curse of a bad set of habits is that all the unnecessary things you're doing actually come to seem necessary.

If the team could stop those calls from coming in, they could reclaim those wasted hours for proactive work. So for 12 business days in a row, they spent one hour "walking the process" from end to end. Noting the way things worked. Spotting problems. Asking questions.

The staff agreed to let Suett shoot video of their operations, and afterward, Suett showed them some clips, like a coach reviewing game film. In one case, a worker had picked up a box five different times before he actually processed it. "Every one of those five steps had a cost," said Suett. "Why don't we just eliminate it? You pick it up once and you process it." The guy had no idea he'd been doing that.

When the team analyzed its own work, they found that only 38% of the time they spent processing packages was "adding value" for the customers they served in the hospital. The rest of it was waste. Spurred on by this recognition, the team started rebuilding the process from top to bottom.

Perhaps the most fundamental change they made was to move

away from "batching" packages. Batching involves performing a single operation on (in this case) a pile of packages before moving on. So maybe one person would put a label on 10 packages, then put them on a cart and roll them to the next area, where somebody else would log them into the computer, and so on. Batching seemed intuitive. Surely it would be inefficient to deal with one package at a time?

But batching caused needless delays. To help his team see this, Suett led an exercise. He asked 10 staffers to sit at a long table, 5 on each side, and challenged the two sides to compete. The goal? To get every person to sign their name on five sticky notes as quickly as possible.

There was a twist: On one side of the table, each person would write their name on all five notes, then pass the stack to the next person. (That's a batch process.) On the other side of the table, the first person would write their name on one note, immediately pass it on, then write their name on the second note, and so on.

The staffers quickly caught on: With the second process, everyone ended up writing simultaneously. Nobody was idle. The notes flowed down the line, steadily, from person to person. It was far faster than the batch process. "It was an eye opener for everybody," said Charles Shipley, one of the workers. "He won a lot of people over with that experiment. It was very convincing."*

Afterward, they began to overhaul the batch processes, eliminating unnecessary steps and moving toward a more continuous operation. Suett's mantra was: *Keep the river flowing.*

And it flowed. Within six weeks, the unthinkable had happened:

---

*Just want to be clear that batching isn't always a bad thing. Like most things, it depends. In the receiving area, it was problematic, but please don't conclude you should wash your clothes one item at a time for the sake of "flow."

90% of the hospital locations were receiving daily deliveries. Again the picture told the story (see above).

An astonished hospital executive brought a group of colleagues to the receiving bay to witness the transformation. And the effects rippled throughout the hospital. As people gained trust in the receiving team, they stopped ordering shipments directly to their departments. They stopped overordering, knowing they'd be able to replenish supplies in a timely manner.

The total estimated cost savings from unclogging the system was over $20 million, according to a case study written by John Nicholas, Hussam Bachour, and Suett.

The red phone stopped ringing.

Many years later, the receiving area continues to hum along efficiently.

Every system is perfectly designed to get the results it gets.

2.

In the fall of 2021, I went to Chick-fil-A to fetch dinner for my family, and unexpectedly, I came home with a book idea. (Also, more expectedly, some fries and nuggets.) I was so awestruck by the efficiency of the drive-thru—you'll hear all about it in chapter 4—that I started researching the question: How do you make things run better?

Eventually, though, I realized that the idea of "better" didn't really capture what I was after. "Better" could be any performance improvement: say, an Olympic swimmer shaving a hundredth of a second off their already stellar race time. Rather, I found myself gravitating toward situations where people were bogged down. These were not "crisis" situations. They were more like bad equilibria: situations that were unsatisfactory and self-sustaining. Kind of like the hospital receiving area.

Surely we're all familiar with situations like this. All of us get stuck sometimes, and it's easy to see why. We're stifled by the gravity of the way we've always done things (*inertia*). We consider so many potential possibilities for change that it freezes us (*decision paralysis*). We spend so much time fighting with colleagues about what we *should* do that we never actually accomplish anything (*politics*). And we exhaust ourselves chasing today's problems, which always seem to crowd out tomorrow's opportunities (*firefighting*).

The question is: How do we reset things? How do we change what's not working?

For about two and a half years, I chased answers to those questions. The principles ahead are drawn from: 240 interviews from people in countless different industries. An exploration of relevant findings from psychology and other disciplines. And a deep dive on certain methodologies that shine at helping people overcome inertia and make progress within short timeframes: agile and scrum, solutions-focused therapy, the incident command system, kaizen events, design sprints, business turnarounds, rapid results projects, and more.

Let's start at the beginning.

When you're stuck, it's like your path is blocked by a boulder. It needs moving, but how could you possibly move it? It's too big. "We need to deliver all the packages we receive within a day." *Well, sure, that would be lovely, but we have NEVER DONE THAT, so what makes you think that is possible?* It feels overwhelming.

Often, we make the mistake of thinking that we're mired down because of a lack of effort. Notice that a lack of effort wasn't the problem in the receiving area—it probably took *more* effort to sustain the bad system, because of all those calls to the red phone.

In other words, you can't just hurl yourself at the boulder. "Shoving harder" is not a viable plan (unless your plan is to slip a disc).

To move the boulder, you need to be smart and strategic. Because of the complexity you face, you can't change everything. You can't change *most* things. You can't even change a respectable fraction of things! But, with a bit of prodding and catalyzing, you can change *something*. A well-chosen something. We'll call that "well-chosen something" a Leverage Point (a term popularized by the systems theorist Donella Meadows).

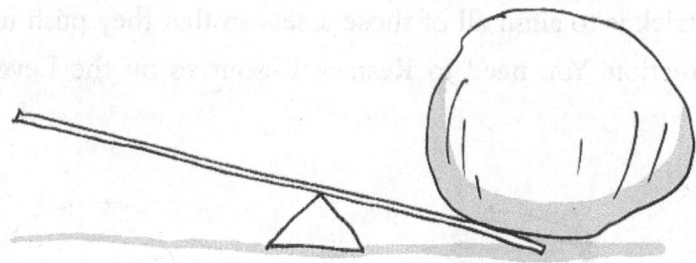

Leverage Points are interventions where a little bit of effort yields disproportionate returns. Of the universe of things you *could* do to improve a situation, the Leverage Points are the things you *should* do. In the hospital receiving area, for instance, one of the key Leverage Points was moving away from batch processes.

Without a Leverage Point, you'll never transform how you work. In the picture above, the Leverage Point is the fulcrum that supports the lever.* But it's not *sufficient* to move the boulder. The boulder hasn't moved yet. To actually move it, you need to apply some resources to the other end of that lever.

Where do you get those resources? Well, right now, you and your team have a wealth of resources—time, money, enthusiasm, processes, etc.—that are being used in various ways.

The trick is to align all of those assets so that they push in the same direction. You need to Restack Resources on the Leverage Point.

---

*Probably the less literal we make this analogy, the better. I'm no physicist. Just roll with me here.

And that's the core framework we'll unpack in this book: To make things happen, you should Find Leverage Points and Restack Resources to push on those points.

Simple, eh? Just do those two things and—POOF—change will flourish!

Well, yes, it can be that simple—but first comes some legwork. To start, you'll be searching for points of intervention where small investments yield big returns. How do you spot those magical Leverage Points, exactly? If they were easy to find, you likely would have found them already. (For years, it didn't occur to the hospital receiving area to move away from batch processing.)

We'll spend the first section of the book on the essential detective work of Finding Leverage Points, covering five methods for locating them:

→ Go and see the work (*in chapter 1*): Observe up close the reality of your work.

→ Consider the goal of the goal (*in chapter 2*): Identify alternate pathways to your ultimate destination.

→ Study the bright spots (*in chapter 3*): Analyze and replicate your own best work.

→ Target the constraint (*in chapter 4*): Assess the #1 force that is holding you back.

→ Map the system (*in chapter 5*): Rise above the silos to spot promising targets for action.

Then, in the second section, we'll turn our attention to Restacking Resources, a quest that comes with its own challenges. The chief obstacle is that you almost certainly don't have a bunch of unused assets that you can mobilize to support your change. You have what you have. And that means if you want to press harder on a Leverage Point, then you need to draw resources from *something else you're doing.*

To spark change, we shouldn't think AND, we should think IN-STEAD OF. Less of this, more of that.

And those trade-offs are painful. Probably no one on your team, today, believes that what they're doing is pointless and therefore their energies can be repurposed in a new direction. So where do you find resources to pile up on Leverage Points when all of those resources are presently committed to something else?

We'll explore six strategies for marshalling resources while minimizing the sting of the trade-offs involved. Here's how you can Restack Resources:

→ Start with a burst (*in chapter 6*): Begin with an intense and focused period of work.

→ Recycle waste (*in chapter 7*): Discontinue efforts that don't serve the mission.

→ Do less AND more (*in chapter 8*): Shift resources from lower-value work to higher-value.

→ Tap motivation (*in chapter 9*): Prioritize the work that's required *and* desired.

→ Let people drive (*in chapter 10*): Give your team the autonomy to lead the change efforts.

→ Accelerate learning (*in chapter 11*): Get better, faster feedback to guide your work.

As you apply this framework, you'll likely encounter powerful obstacles: tradition and resistance and bureaucracy and indifference. But if you can manage to move the boulder—even by just a few inches—you'll find there's a powerful force in your favor. And it's one you might not expect.

Consider a study conducted by Teresa Amabile and Steven Kramer. They were interested in employees' "inner work life," meaning their "thoughts, feelings, and drives triggered by the events of the workday." To trace these everyday emotions, Amabile and Kramer asked employees to keep daily diaries reflecting on their work. Eventually, 238 employees across 7 companies submitted over 12,000 diary reports.

What emerged from these diaries was a crystal-clear finding that the researchers called the *progress principle*: "Of all the things that can boost emotions, motivation, and perceptions during a workday, the single most important is making progress in meaningful work." According to the employee diaries, 76% of people's best days involved progress; only 13% of their best days involved setbacks.

Progress energized people and made them happy. Setbacks did the opposite. No other work dynamics had as dramatic an effect on employees' inner life.

What's particularly striking about the research, as Amabile and Kramer chronicle in their book *The Progress Principle*, is that most bosses were oblivious to the value of progress as a motivator. "When we surveyed managers around the world and asked them to rank employee motivators in terms of importance, only 5% chose progress as #1," said Amabile in a speech. "Progress came in dead last."

It's a stunning oversight: The biggest motivator of employees is nowhere on the radar of the average boss.

But you can overcome that mistake. Progress will be your secret weapon, the way it was for Paul Suett at Northwestern Memorial Hospital. He showed his team how to make things better: *You don't have to pick up the box five times. You don't have to batch the packages. Let the river flow.*

And they responded! It was their work and their enthusiasm that ultimately transformed the department, not his. Frank Marasso was a leader in the group. He spent most of his career—42 years and counting—in the receiving area. He said, "The minute we actually got our FedEx and UPS packages—all 600 pieces—worked up and delivered, and that room's empty at the end of the day? I was like, 'Yeah, this is cool.'" He admitted he was skeptical of Suett's ideas at first. But the results made him a believer: "An empty room is a beautiful thing, man."

This transformation did not require a huge infusion of new people or new assets. It was the same staff in the same space with the same goal they'd always had: to process and deliver packages for a hospital. But after carefully reimagining their work, they went from "pariahs" to superstars.

In the chapters ahead, we'll explore how other groups faced down their own daunting obstacles: A library on the cusp of collapse. A public company losing a dangerous number of clients. A marriage fraying at the seams. A hospital with burned-out and disengaged staffers.

All of them, as you'll see, moved the boulder.

We'll encounter cases involving military planes, music apps, radiology clinics, church services, car dealerships, and archery competitions. We'll investigate mysteries: Why the middle is the roughest part of a change effort. Why *inefficiency* can sometimes accelerate progress. Why "getting buy-in" is the wrong way to think about change. Why people may think they understand the systems they depend on better than they actually do. (Spoiler on that last one: Realizing this can be shocking to the people involved—see the next chapter for more.)

You'll also learn how five million cats' lives were saved, and perhaps most dramatically of all, how one father got his kids to clean their room. With enthusiasm.

Ultimately, the payoffs for our exploration ahead are simple but powerful: The relief of shaking off bad habits. The pleasure of experiencing movement where stasis had prevailed. The sudden snap of agency that comes from reminding yourself: *I'm capable of changing this situation.*

Yesterday, we were spinning our wheels. Today, we reset and start rolling forward.*

HOORAY!

---

*A huge thank-you to my friend and fellow business author Jake Knapp, who came up with the idea for the boulder/lever/fulcrum artwork and contributed the drawings. I love what they add to the book and I'm grateful!

SECTION 1

FIND LEVERAGE POINTS

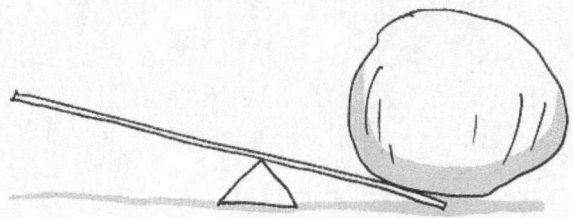

 **Chapter 1: Go and see the work**

 **Chapter 2: Consider the goal of the goal**

 **Chapter 3: Study the bright spots**

 **Chapter 4: Target the constraint**

 **Chapter 5: Map the system**

SECTION 1

FIND LEVERAGE POINTS

1

GO AND SEE THE WORK

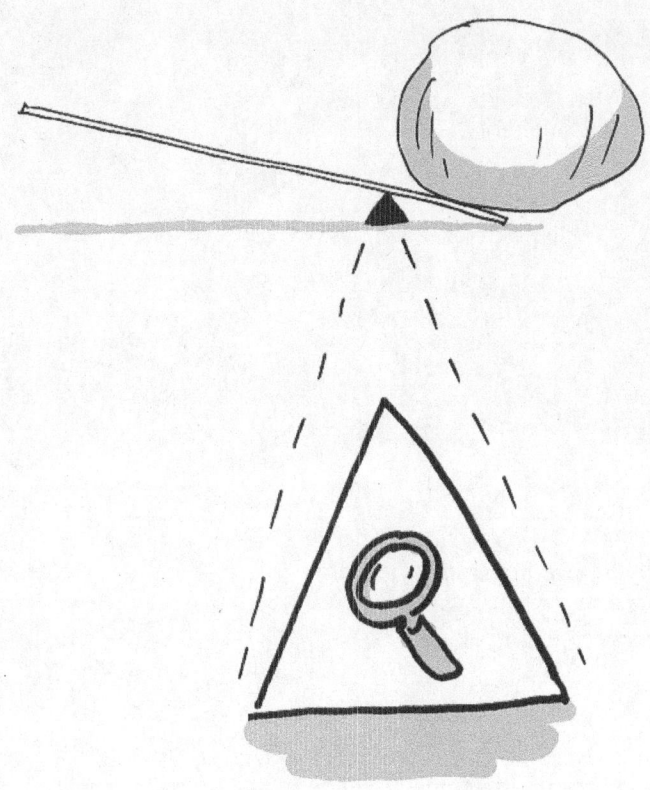

>> You can Find Leverage Points by observing
up close the reality of your work.

GO AND SEE THE WORK

1.

In 2016, Karen Ritter, an assistant principal at East Leyden High School (near Chicago), wanted to understand how the school could better serve its students. So she chose to do something unorthodox. As part of a program called "Shadow a Student Challenge," created by the Stanford d.school and the design firm IDEO, she followed around a ninth-grader, Alan, for an entire school day.

Her day with Alan started in PE. She gamely ran sprints in the gym while students gawked and grinned. Afterward, the academic school day began. She sat next to him in class. Completed assignments, just like he did. Ate cafeteria food. ("Lunch was difficult," she said diplomatically.)

Ritter's experience was covered by PBS for a news segment, and watching the video of Ritter's day is a bit like watching a balloon deflate in slow motion. At one point, the journalist asks her how she's doing. "I'm holding up," she says with a strained smile. (Body language: *I am not holding up*.)

Particularly draining was Alan's algebra class. Because of his low test scores in math, he'd been slotted into a double-length remedial period. The camera caught Ritter sneaking looks at the clock, just like a real student. After a long stretch of instruction, the bell rang, but to Ritter's chagrin, it wasn't for her. There were 30 more minutes to go. "It was brutal to sit through that," she said.

The day before her observation, Ritter was asked to complete a report card, grading the school on a variety of factors. For "Supportive Environment," she gave the school an A. Then, after her day of shadowing, she was asked to revisit those marks.

The grade for Supportive Environment stayed an A: She was pleased with what she experienced. But on other factors, the grades deteriorated. Before the day, she'd scored the school a B on this statement: "In this school, students learn actively, creating, questioning, discovering." After her day as a student, the B cratered to a C-minus.

Similarly, with the grinding double-length algebra class fresh in her mind, her score for "Student Engagement" dropped from a B to a C-plus.

By shadowing a student, Ritter discovered that some of her intuitions had been exactly right. The school really did provide a supportive environment. In other places, though, her intuition had been way off the mark.

	Before	After
SUPPORTIVE ENVIRONMENT	A	A
ACTIVE LEARNING	B	C-
STUDENT ENGAGEMENT	B	C+

She wondered about the double-length math period, for instance. "We don't have proof that this is improving [students'] learning," she said. "It's just making them more miserable." For Alan, the double-length class had crowded out his real interests. He had wanted to take classes in French and automotive skills, but he couldn't do both. (Other students were able to pick two electives.)

Ritter's goal, in shadowing a student, was to look for ways to improve the student experience. Her day with Alan had helped her identify two potential Leverage Points: (1) reconsidering the automatic slotting of students into double-length remedial periods; and (2) encouraging faculty to be more interactive in their classrooms. The school would later act upon both of these ideas: The faculty received professional development in better engaging students, and the school subsequently changed its policy to ensure that every student could have at least one elective. (Previously, some kids who had both a double-reading and a double-math course had no choice at all in their schedule!)

In this section, we'll explore five methods for identifying Leverage Points. Finding them will require some detective work: Sometimes they are hidden—masked by habits or assumptions. Other times (as we'll see on the next few pages), they can be quite obvious to anyone who looks. Either way, *we have to go looking*—and we have to know where to look. The tools in this section will give us five independent ways to conduct the hunt.

What we're looking for are interventions that are both *doable* and *worth doing*. "Doable": meaning that they are possible in the short term. And "worth doing": because we aspire to move boulders, not pebbles.

The first method for finding Leverage Points is the one used by Ritter, an approach that Nelson Repenning calls "Go and see the work."* Repenning is a professor at MIT who studies system dynamics. He told me that of all the principles he's shared with executives and students over the years, the one that most reliably pays off is: *Go and see the work.*

Meaning: If you're a school principal, shadow a student for the day. If you're a factory manager, follow the production from start to finish. If you're a consultant, map out the flow of activities on a single client engagement.

"Going and seeing the work" is what the hospital receiving area team did when they began their overhaul: They followed packages through the system, from the delivery dock to their ultimate destinations in the hospital.

One executive, following Repenning's imperative to see the work, discovered that in his company, there was a woman who diligently maintained a repository of the firm's engineering documents. She spent long stretches of time printing high-definition color prints and organizing them in a room full of file cabinets.

But there was a digital repository that auto-archived these files. It had existed for years. And word never got back to this poor woman.

"When you go see the work," wrote Repenning and two colleagues, Don Kieffer and Todd Astor, "if you aren't embarrassed by what you find, you probably aren't looking closely enough."†

---

*Repenning's phrasing is a riff on a well-known operations concept called "going to the gemba," which originated with Taiichi Ohno, the godfather of the Toyota Production System. "Gemba" comes from a Japanese term meaning the "actual place."

†Note that this spirit of examination—the genuine desire to get closer to the truth—is the heart of "going and seeing the work." This is in sharp contrast to the CEO who conducts a stage-managed visit to a factory or field office for the sake of good optics: *I am an enlightened leader who enjoys mingling with you common folk!*

Repenning, Kieffer, and Michael Morales published a revealing case study in *MIT Sloan Management Review*. Morales, the president of a Panama City plant that made corrugated boxes, wanted to understand why his paper losses during production were higher than the industry average. So he went to see the work. And the authors reported what happened next:

Mike left his office and visited the factory floor to watch the work and understand its current design. He quickly observed numerous problems. The paper was often too wide, resulting in extra losses from cutting. In addition, paper rolls were often damaged by the forklifts that moved them . . .

Perhaps most notably, Mike observed that the main corrugator machine stopped at 11:30am. Assuming it was an unplanned outage, Mike rushed to the machine only to learn that the machine was stopped *every day* at lunch. Stopping and restarting the machine at lunchtime not only decreased productivity but also increased the probability of both damage to paper and mechanical problems. Interestingly, the lunch break turned out to be a response that had been instituted years ago in response to instability in the electric power provided by the local utility—a problem that had been fixed long ago.

Morales's investigation, then, surfaced some obvious Leverage Points for whittling down paper waste. Within two months, paper losses fell from 21% to 15%, reflecting a savings of $50,000.

Now, your first reaction to this story might be: *Well, sure, if you're doing stuff that's obviously dumb/wrong, then you can easily fix the dumb/wrong stuff.* But be careful: Repenning and Kieffer wrote, "We have discovered similarly 'obvious' issues in almost every piece of work we have ever studied. . . ."

Glaring problems are sometimes the legacy of past *solutions*—improvisations and workarounds. Take the case of the paper plant: As the plant manager, you observe that you're getting unsteady power to your corrugating machine around lunchtime. It's not good for efficiency, and it's not good for the machine itself. So you schedule a shutdown every day to preserve the equipment. That's proactive and wise. A great short-term solution.

But of course you'll never get an official announcement from the utility saying, "All Clear!" so the daily shutdown continues. Weeks become months, months become years, and habits become enshrined. Your plant depends on so many habits for its basic functioning that eventually you stop distinguishing them individually, and rather they just collectively become The Way We Do Things. A new employee, learning the ropes, is taught: Every day, at lunchtime, we shut down the corrugating machine.

So what looks like "mismanagement" is often the accidental accretion of outdated habits. And the way you can begin to detect and ultimately erode that accretion is by *going and seeing the work*. You'll spot places where you and your team have acclimated to problems—instead of fixing them. Those long-tolerated bad habits are Leverage Points: Correcting them is doable and worth doing.

For knowledge work, this type of observation can be harder. You can trace a corrugated box through a factory. But can you trace, say, the development of a market analysis by a consulting firm?

Yes. For sure, yes. But it's not as tangible. You will have to make it tangible by mapping out the flow: *Okay, for the Kipon Trucking account, we first had the kickoff meeting (two hours), and then we prepared a research plan (six days), which we sent to the client, who returned feedback (two days), and then the engagement manager gave assignments to the five core team members (one day), and then . . .*

You're making the invisible visible. Think whiteboards and

markers. How long does each step take? Where does work get stuck or delayed? How do communications ping-pong between the team and the client? In what steps do the greatest leaps forward seem to happen? Protect those. And in what steps do the efforts seem to add little value? Rework or eliminate those.

In short, you can still *go and see the work*.

The key thing here—and the radical departure from normal, everyday work—is that you are substituting experience for conjecture. Tom Chi, a co-founder of X, the ambitious R & D lab at Google, said that most corporate decisions are made using "guess-a-thons." People sit around and duel in the land of ideas.

A sample meeting: Ted thinks you should try the Bold Strategy. Marisa hates Ted, so she pushes back on it. Helen, anxious about making decisions, always suggests waiting for more data. Gregg is always a hair's breadth away from making a strained face and asking *How will it affect the CULTURE?* (Gregg is everyone's least favorite part of the culture.)

And on and on it goes. Ultimately, as Chi said in a workshop, "Either the person who is best at arguing or the person with the highest title in the room ends up deciding." The tragedy, of course, is that when you make decisions that way, you've made important decisions based on cognitive vapor.

"Smart people will always come up with smart reasons for their guesses," said Chi. "But that does not mean that their guesses are not guesses. . . . Because it actually doesn't matter how much you agree or disagree—if it sounds smart or doesn't sound smart. The only thing to listen for is: When I hear something, is it a guess or is it a direct experience? If it's a guess, it needs to be treated a certain way. . . . But if it's a direct experience, then that's the stuff we want to make decisions off of."

Chi's challenge to us is to get out of the "medium of guesses" and into the medium of reality. When we go and see the work, we stop debating ideas and start discovering them.

2.

Going and seeing the work can be particularly important when things stop working. Your marriage hits a rocky patch. Your sales start drying up. Teachers leave your school faster than you can replace them.

Because when unexpected problems arise in our organizations, it often reveals that we didn't know as much about our "system" as we thought we did.

On this point, consider a study by the psychologists Leonid Rozenblit and Frank Keil, who asked people to assess how well they understood certain familiar devices. *How well do you understand how a zipper works? A flush toilet?* People reported moderate levels of understanding. On a seven-point scale, with seven reflecting the highest level of understanding, the average score landed a bit under four.

After the participants scored themselves, Rozenblit and Keil put them to the test: *Okay, write out a step-by-step explanation of how the device works, from the first step to the last. Feel free to draw pictures to get your meaning across.*

There's a great YouTube video that brings this study to life. A teenager named Alex Nickel, inspired by the research, asked some teenage peers to explain how a toilet works. Their answers were memorable:

> TEEN 1: Well, so there's a handle, and you flush it, and it goes
> through some machinery . . .

TEEN 2: There's like pipes going up to the top thing, and then you press the flusher thing, and then the water goes all around and it flushes the gross stuff out . . .

ALEX NICKEL: How does that actually, like, flush it out?

TEEN 2: It goes down a pipe? I don't know.

TEEN 3: Water comes out into the bowl and, like, PUSHES the stuff down . . .

ALEX NICKEL: Can you elaborate on that? Like, the pushing?

TEEN 3: Um, I'm not sure.

To get back to the original study: After the participants had finished their "explanations" of the device, they were asked to rate their understanding of the device for a second time.

Their self-assessments plummeted.

"Nearly all participants showed drops in estimates of what they knew," wrote Rozenblit and Keil in their 2002 study. The psychologists called this the "illusion of explanatory depth." As they wrote, "Most people feel they understand the world with far greater detail, coherence, and depth than they really do." When participants were prodded to produce an explanation, they realized, *I know a lot less than I thought.*

In another study of this illusion, conducted by Rebecca Lawson and published in *Memory and Cognition*, people were presented with this skeletal picture of a bicycle frame and asked to add pedals, a chain, and the remaining parts of the frame to the sketch:

(Before you look down, pause. Could you do this exercise correctly? How confident are you?)

One person drew a bike like this. Take a second to analyze what's wrong here.

One problem: This bike won't move; the pedals aren't attached to any moving part of the system. And look how high the pedals are! Are people supposed to pedal with their kneecaps?

Here was another participant's bike:

At first glance, this looks pretty fancy. Spokes and hand brakes were added, unsolicited, for extra realism! But notice the chain and the frame are connecting both wheels. Which means this bike can't be turned. It's a one-way ticket to the emergency room.

Here's one more point of interest about that last bike: The person who drew it reported that *they went cycling most days*. (Presumably in a straight line?)

I'm poking fun but let me confess: I had to look up the answer about how a bike works. I'm pretty sure I would have drawn the chain around both wheels, too.

So I'm inclined to empathize with the cyclist. After all, you don't need to *understand* the bike to use it effectively! Isn't a functional understanding sufficient?

The problem comes when we mistake *functional* understanding for *systemic* understanding. We think because we can *use* something, because it operates as we expect, that we understand it. And that's a problem, because when the bike or the zipper or the toilet stops working, we're sunk. We realize that underneath our functional level of understanding, there's nothing.

3.

That sudden awakening is what befalls many businesses just as they are plunged into crisis. Businesses struggle, and their leaders think, *It'll turn around. Just wait a little longer. I've run this place for 10 years. We've been through hard times.*

But then, sometimes, things don't turn around. And because dramatic action wasn't taken earlier, when it was a choice, it becomes mandatory. Change or go bankrupt.

In those situations—when a business is in danger of failing—investors or board members might hire a "turnaround consultant." That's someone who parachutes into the company, takes over the place, makes a bunch of changes, and then leaves after a few months.

Consider how odd this arrangement is. You might think that if your business was in a pickle, you'd *seek advice* from someone with turnaround expertise, the way that you might visit a therapist if your marriage was foundering. This isn't that. This is handing over the reins to a stranger. It's like letting the therapist *move in with your spouse*, fix the relationship, then turn it back over to you.*

Despite the dire circumstances involved—businesses on the brink of bankruptcy—turnarounds frequently succeed. We're used to thinking about organizational change as slow. But, no, in these situations, a company might be rescued—from life support to basic health—in a matter of months.

So let's think like a turnaround consultant. You're coming into a company that once was viable and now isn't. This predicament triggers the shift from functional to systemic understanding (as in the toilet and bike examples above). Things were working, now they aren't. How do you quickly make sense of what's wrong and how to fix it?

Turnaround consultants *go and see the work*.† They walk the halls, they observe the production lines. But because they aren't experts in the particular business they're now running, the observation is not enough. They need guidance. So in trying to understand the reality of a business, turnaround artists go straight to the front lines.

"If you really want to know what's going on in an organization, you always ask the people closest to the customer and closest to the core activity, whether it's providing a service or making something," said the turnaround consultant Paul Fioravanti on a podcast.

Jeff Vogelsang, a turnaround consultant with Promontory Point Partners, seconds the approach. "I go to people and say, 'This is a private conversation. I'm not gonna share anything you say. I'm looking for common themes. I'm looking for your opinions. . . .'

"And they'll say, 'I don't care. I'll tell you everything. They can

---

*Could someone start working on BODY turnaround consultants? Just call me when my six-pack is ready.

†Wait, never mind about the "body turnaround" thing . . .

fire me.' Then they'll puke out everything that has gone on, everything that's wrong. I'll write 10 pages of notes, 90% of it turns out to be accurate and 10% is emotional or a personal grudge. . . . Within two weeks, the people who work there will tell you what's going on, if you're good at asking open questions and shutting up and letting them ramble."

As a methodology, this could not be simpler: To find out what's going on in your organization, talk to the people who make it run. *Here's what customers really think of us. Here's why our plant is so messed up. Here's why the software updates are always late.*

There's no black magic. It's just listening.

Parenthetically, when I've shared this idea with people, I sometimes get a polarized reaction. Some people have a cynical attitude: *Frontline people are just clock-punchers. If I ask them what's wrong, they're gonna say they work too hard or they don't get paid enough.* And others have an overly romantic view: *Yes, power to the front lines! They do all the hard work and nobody listens to them! They could run the place better than the suits!*

I sometimes wonder whether either group (cynical or romantic) has actually met any frontline people. Because the truth is, they're just people. They have smart ideas and dumb ideas. The advice is not: *Consult them because they're wise, selfless oracles.* The advice is: *Consult them because they know their jobs better than you, and their jobs are closer to reality than yours.*

Going and seeing the work, ultimately, is about observation and consultation.

I see we turn off the corrugating machine every day. Why do we do that?

We thought we were helping students with a double-length remedial math course, but is there any proof it's working? Or are we just doubling their suffering?

The payoff for this observational effort can be profound. Imagine if you could locate and stop the dumbest things your team is doing: the ill-advised, the pointless, the self-sabotaging—BOOM, gone. What would that be worth?

There are unmistakable areas for improvement that we may never see and brilliant ideas for change that we'll never unlock unless we *go and see the work.*

Whirlwind review: Chapter 1, Go and See the Work

1. The first way to identify Leverage Points is to observe our work more closely. As Nelson Repenning says, "Go and see the work."
   a. *Assistant Principal Karen Ritter uncovered some hard truths about her school by shadowing a student.*

2. When you go and see the work, you often discover that you've been oblivious to problems, or have acclimated to them, instead of fixing them.
   a. *The president of the paper plant discovered that the corrugating machine was being shut down every day at lunch—because of an energy problem that had been resolved years earlier.*
   b. *Mismanagement is often the accidental accretion of outdated habits.*

3. Going and seeing the work is far preferable to the usual conference-room style of hatching improvements—what Tom Chi calls "guess-a-thons."
   a. *To find real Leverage Points, you must get out of the medium of guesses and into the medium of reality.*

4. When you're trying to improve your work, you'll often discover that you have *functional* understanding rather than *systemic* understanding. Without that systemic understanding, it's hard to make things better.
   a. *Even regular cyclists couldn't draw a bicycle accurately. That's the "illusion of explanatory depth."*

5. But it's possible to gain systemic understanding quickly. Turnaround consultants do it by going straight to the front lines.
   a. *"The people who work there will tell you what's going on" if you shut up and let them talk.*

6. Ultimately, going and seeing the work is about getting closer to the reality of the situation and perceiving it with fresh eyes. That's how you find promising Leverage Points.

Recommendations (find live links at <u>danheath.com/reset-links</u>):

(Note from Dan Heath: Here's a quick explanation of these "Recommendations" sections that follow each chapter. These are not sources per se—the endnotes are at the back of the book. Rather, the Recommendations offer tips about places to explore beyond the book. Sometimes the links give extra color to the points made in the text; sometimes they're the original sources cited, when I think those sources are worth a deeper dive; sometimes they're interesting tangents. The "links" are underlined below but please know that I am not an insane person who thinks you can poke your finger at them to visit a website. The idea here is that you should visit the website <u>danheath.com/reset-links</u> and there you'll find this exact paragraph below, except that the links will be clickable. Happy hunting!)

<u>In this talk</u>, which I highly recommend, the engineer and innovator Tom Chi describes how he fights against guess-a-thons and gets his teams working in the medium of reality. To see what it's like for a principal to step into the reality of a student, <u>watch the *PBS NewsHour* segment</u> I mention in the chapter. You'll see Assistant Principal Karen Ritter run sprints, battle back-to-back sections of Algebra, and write an essay alongside her ninth-grade shadowee, Alan Garcia. If you'd like to take a deeper look at the illusion of explanatory depth research, <u>head here for the academic article</u>. (And to see that video of teenagers struggling to explain toilets, <u>go here</u>.) If you're curious about the swashbuckling world of turnaround specialists, start with James Shein's <u>*Reversing the Slide*</u>. Shein's book is both sharp and irreverent, making for an engaging read. Or, take a listen to my conversation with the turnaround consultant Jeff Vogelsang, whom I interviewed on <u>my podcast, *What It's Like to Be . . .*</u> He's the guy quoted in this chapter saying that when you interview frontline people, they'll "puke out" everything that was relevant. For more on "going to the gemba"—the inspiration for MIT professor Nelson Repenning's "go and see the work" advice—check out <u>*The Toyota Way*</u>. It's a great summary of the Toyota Production System—much beloved by operations gurus. In <u>this article</u> and <u>this talk</u>, Repenning details how you can increase the visibility of the work you and your team are doing. This is especially important for knowledge work, Repenning points out, where feedback is naturally far less visible than in manufacturing.

CONSIDER THE GOAL
OF THE GOAL

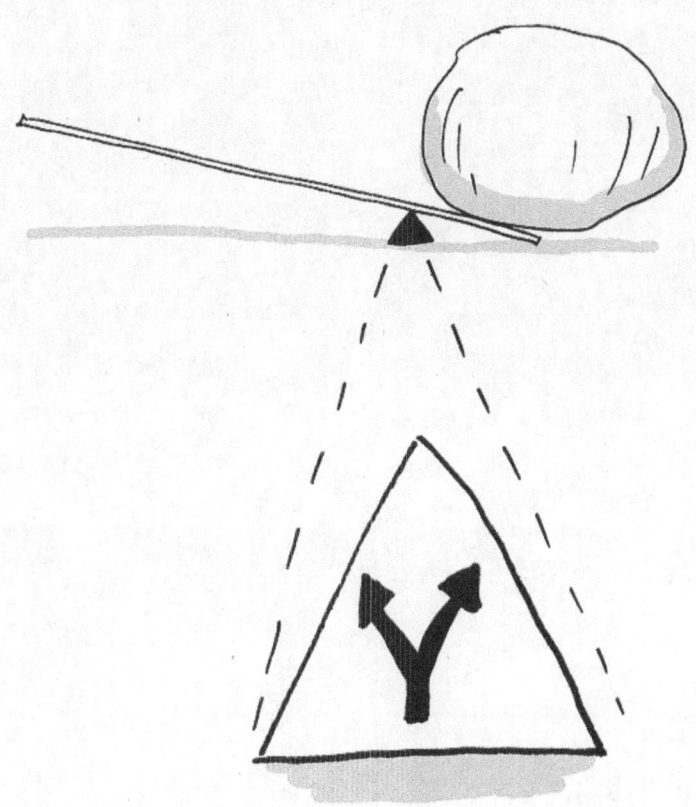

>> You can Find Leverage Points by identifying alternate pathways to your ultimate destination.

CONSIDER THE GOAL
OF THE GOAL

1.

On July 15, 2022, Ryan Davidsen bought a new pickup truck. A Ram 1500. To celebrate, he planned to take it on a camping trip the next weekend.

Then, a few days after he drove it off the lot, the survey shakedown began.

The dealership texted him on July 20 asking for a rating from 0 to 10 on the "overall buying experience." He texted back a 9.

On July 21, Brittany—a customer care assistant—emailed him, asking, "Is there anything that we could have done better?" The next day, a Friday, she sent another email, wondering, "How could we have made your experience more pleasant?" The next Monday, undeterred by his nonresponse, she sent a third email: "There is just one thing that we would like to know. How could your purchasing experience have been better?"

That same Monday, another person from the dealership, Megan, texted him to see whether he needed anything. And his salesperson texted, too:

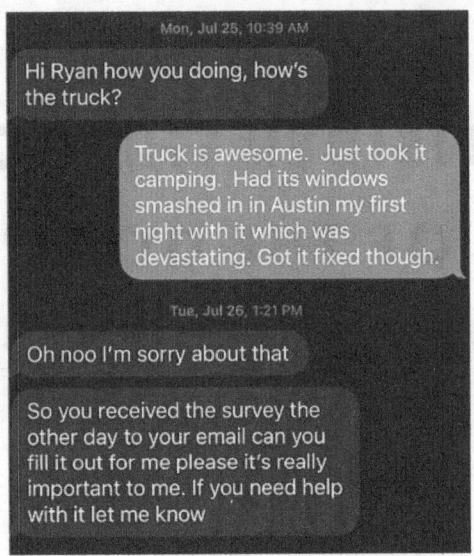

Mon, Jul 25, 10:39 AM

Hi Ryan how you doing, how's the truck?

Truck is awesome. Just took it camping. Had its windows smashed in in Austin my first night with it which was devastating. Got it fixed though.

Tue, Jul 26, 1:21 PM

Oh noo I'm sorry about that

So you received the survey the other day to your email can you fill it out for me please it's really important to me. If you need help with it let me know

(You get the sense that if a loved one died, the salesperson would send flowers and a survey.)

On Wednesday, the dealership texted him again, stating "our team would really appreciate your positive responses."

Davidsen could sympathize with the dealership's desire for feedback, because at the time he was in charge of customer experience for a health care software firm. He, too, had to keep tabs on customer satisfaction. He could relate.

So, he took the time to fill out the survey. Gave some high scores, some low, reflecting his experience. He left thoughtful comments so the dealership could understand his ratings. He also replied to Brittany, who'd been desperate for that "one thing" that would have improved his experience.

He wrote, "I liked the people I worked with—my salesperson and my finance specialist. They were easy to work with and made it an enjoyable experience." Then he elaborated on what could have gone better:

> Things I didn't like was the experience of seeing all of the additional items that get added to the final purchase price that I then have to negotiate out or negotiate down with a lot of back-and-forth as everyone had to check with a higher-up while I wait. I hated that.

Still, he concluded on a positive note: "I'd buy from you again and intend to stick with this dealership for service. Thanks for asking."

He never heard from Brittany again.

Within hours of submitting his survey, his salesperson texted him again: "Hey Ryan did I do anything wrong? I got a low score." Davidsen wrote back, "Not at all—had nothing but great things to say about you. I hope they let you read it." The salesperson replied: "I understand that but every single score mattered."

Since then, Davidsen said, the dealership "lost" the paperwork on the bed cover he bought with his truck. "Two months later I still don't have a bed cover and every text and email I sent have gone unanswered, which leaves me feeling it is 'payback' for the fair and helpful survey I sent," he said.

2.

Let's lift our view of Davidsen's horror story to the systems level. Because this is a story of change gone wrong. Badly wrong.

The leaders at Stellantis (the multinational that owns Dodge, Chrysler, Jeep, and Ram) were surely not intending to produce stories like this one. No doubt their original intent was pretty respectable: *We want to create a great car-buying experience for our customers!* That mission is big, long-term, and somewhat diffuse. What kind of shorter-term goal might serve that long-term mission? *Boosting customer-satisfaction scores.*

And my guess is that the team at the dealership where Davidsen bought his truck did, in fact, make progress toward that short-term goal. Probably their customer-satisfaction scores were outstanding! But their success was due not to their passion for improving the customer experience but rather to their prowess at browbeating customers into providing falsely inflated scores. That's a sad kind of excellence.*

If you were a senior brand leader at Ram, you'd surely want to sniff out this discrepancy. How could you do it? By *going and seeing the work.* The problems that Ryan Davidsen experienced were not subtle at all. (I mean, his salesperson responded to his text about having his brand-new truck's windows bashed in by saying, *Aw man, bummer, but anyhoo, about that survey . . .*) But to spot problems—even obvious ones—you do have to look.

All it would have taken, to surface silly antics like the dealership's, was a single in-person visit—perhaps by someone posing as

---

*And for even sadder excellence: When Davidsen was still in the process of buying his truck, the sales rep brought over a FRAMED version of the survey that Davidsen would eventually be asked to fill out. The sales rep walked him through every question on it and *told him what the "right" answer to each question should be!* On the question "How would you rate your sales consultant overall?" he instructed Davidsen to give him a 10 out of 10. (The sales rep also thoughtfully gave Davidsen a laminated take-home copy of the survey, with right answers filled in, for further study and reflection.) All of these maneuvers provide a killer illustration of Goodhart's Law: "When a measure becomes a target, it ceases to be a good measure."

a potential customer. That visit would have revealed that the dealership's actual behavior was making a mockery of its mission. At that point, surely the leaders would have realized: *We're moving the numbers, but they're the wrong numbers.*

You should embrace the same discipline in your own change efforts: Before you strain yourself to budge a boulder, it's worth asking: Are you targeting the *right* boulder?

You don't want to fall into the dealership's trap of relentlessly chasing a goal and triumphantly making progress on your measures, only to discover (whoops) that it was all misdirected energy. One simple way to avoid that misalignment—a goal that's inconsistent with the real mission—is to ask a simple but powerful question: *What's the goal of the goal?*

The British advertising guru Rory Sutherland gave a great example of this idea in action. In 2007, Eurostar had finished upgrading the rail route from London to Paris, shaving the travel time from 2 hours 35 minutes to 2 hours 15 minutes. The total price tag was roughly £6 billion, and the goal of the investment had been to speed up the route. Mission accomplished. But what was the *goal of the goal?*

If the goal, ultimately, was to make things better for the passengers, was that investment well spent? Sutherland was dubious. "For 0.01% of this money, you could have put Wi-Fi on the trains, which wouldn't have reduced the duration of the journey, but would have improved its enjoyment and its usefulness far more," he said in a 2011 speech. "For maybe 10% of the money, you could have paid all of the world's top male and female supermodels to walk up and down the train handing out free Château Pétrus to all the passengers. You'd still have five billion pounds in change, and people would ask for the trains to be slowed down."

We can get so fixated on a goal that we miss the bigger picture.

And when we lock into a particular goal too quickly, we blind ourselves to alternate routes forward that might have been better and easier.

In early 2023, I studied a group of people as they set New Year's resolutions and began to work toward them. Marisa Lavars, an Australian mother of two, had initially declared this as her goal: "I'd like to get fit, or fitter. To be able to go about my daily activities without being breathless and to lose a bit of weight so I can fit into my pre-COVID clothes."

Lavars had significant health challenges. She was struggling with heart problems triggered by COVID, and as if that weren't enough, she had recently been diagnosed with breast cancer. Her reference to being "breathless" was no exaggeration: Everyday activities like showering could exhaust her. Her heart rate sometimes spiked to 180 even when she was lying down.

After Lavars submitted her resolution to get fitter, the survey prompted her to consider why that goal was important to her. (In other words, what was the goal of her goal?) Here's what Lavars wrote: "Absolutely my kids. I want to be the best Mum I can be for them and part of that is being healthy, but it also means modeling for them living my best life."

Then, the survey asked her: What are 10 different ways you could achieve or approach that aspiration, other than by following your initial resolution? Suddenly, her answers changed dramatically. Here is what she wrote about her alternate pathways:

→ "Things have been pretty serious for us this past year. I could find some ways to bring back some fun into our lives as fun at times has been in short supply."

→ "We used to have some pretty locked-in routines in the evening, where things stopped and we did some reading, writing, and maths and then I would read to them. This has been pretty pared back or hasn't occurred at all. This would be important to get back to doing."

→ "I would like to bring back music into our lives."

Lavars realized, immediately, that these ideas would get her closer to "success" than the fitness-oriented goals. "I already feel a sense of light-heartedness through going through this process," she wrote. "It feels more connected to the why."

Within a few months, she had dreamed up a variety of ways that she could create moments with her twin seven-year-old boys, despite her poor health. She'd bought some rocking chairs for the veranda. They would sit outside and rock and watch their guinea pigs play. She bought the Harry Potter 6,000-piece LEGO set—they'd been opening one bag of the kit each week.

She had also started a tradition of playing board games. Even at her worst—lying on the couch with an ice pack, trying to bring her heart rate down—she could still participate. She'd call out, "Who's gonna roll the dice?" She'd tease, "Did you cheat?"

"Even if I'm vomiting, I'll still be playing the bloody board game." She laughed. "It just feels really doable. And it's great for the kids too—they're just so much more settled because they know that mum is still mum."

She looks back with amusement on her initial resolution. She had been thinking, "I have to get fit, because I have to spend more time with the kids. . . . I look back now and go, I would never have actually done that, or I would have felt bad about it."

By reconsidering her first goal—and contemplating instead the "goal of the goal"—she was able to ensure that the progress she made *amounted to something meaningful* for herself and her kids.

3.

Another tool for exploring the "goal of the goal" is a technique that comes from the discipline of solutions-focused therapy. It's called the "Miracle Question." The therapist says the following:

> Imagine that in the middle of the night tonight, as you are sleeping, a miracle happens . . . the problem you are stressed about has been solved. Poof! Gone. But the miracle happened when you were sleeping, so when you first wake up, you have no way of knowing it happened.
>
> What are the first things you notice, as you start your day, that reveal to you that the miracle happened?

A therapist named Linda Metcalf asked the Miracle Question to a couple, Elaine and Felix, whose marriage was on the rocks. Here were their answers:

ELAINE: When we were first married, we were best friends. In our miracle we would be best friends again. We would be doing things we did then—dancing, hiking, talking, talking, and more talking.

FELIX: The kids would be better behaved and we would share the responsibility for the kids more equally. Sometimes I think I have to do everything. In the miracle, she wouldn't get on the phone with her sisters at night and we would help the kids with their schoolwork together.

ELAINE: We wouldn't be so resentful and distrusting. Instead we would sit down and plan together for a change, like we used to.

FELIX: I think she's wonderful and I want her to want me

again. In the miracle, she would look up from her book when I came home and be glad to see me.

Think of the magic of this question. Felix and Elaine came to therapy because their marriage was in trouble. It was a fraught emotional situation: big and thorny and depressing. But, in response to the Miracle Question, listen to how they talk: "we would sit down and plan together." "She would look up from her book when I came home." It's a wonderfully tangible vision.

Having answered the question, they now know how to proceed. As the therapist Metcalf said, "[Elaine] never knew that simply glancing up at him when he came in at night would mean so much. He had no idea that she still *would* like to go dancing like they used to." Those are Leverage Points! Small things that could make a big difference.*

The Miracle Question is not just for therapy. In a work setting, it can surface disagreements about your direction. As an example, maybe your boss yammers constantly about being a "customer-centric" organization. But nobody has quite the same understanding of what that means.

So ask the Miracle Question to the team: Okay, we wake up tomorrow and we've *transformed into a customer-centric organization*! What are the first things we notice?

---

*Note that the Miracle Question is not the same as getting wishes from a genie: "In my miracle, I'd win the lottery and my husband would look like George Clooney and my kids would be kind." The question can provide clarity but not magic. It's only the third part of that "wish"—"my kids would be kind"—where the question could realistically provide some traction. What would you notice, behaviorally, if you woke up and your kids had become "kind"? Do you sometimes see those behaviors already, even if infrequently? Are there things that *you* do that seem to elicit those good behaviors? Etc.

I have used this question myself in organizational-change work-shops, and the question can be transformative. But be warned: It usually requires some persistence. Usually, people hem and haw a bit and then leap to how they'd be *feeling*. "I'd be so happy. I'd feel so relieved." That's a good start. But keep redirecting them to the *visible signs of the miracle*. What did you notice that clued you in that something great had happened?

When you steer the conversation toward observations, you ensure that it's tangible enough to flush out any hidden disagreement. One person says: "Well, after the Customer-Centric Miracle happens, hmmm . . . I'd get to work and I'd bump into a group that was leaving HQ to spend time at a customer site, to get to know the customer's problems better." Another chimes in: "Oh, I wasn't thinking about it that way—I was thinking that it was more about cutting internal projects that weren't directly connected to the customer."

Now you have something useful to argue about! Because in the absence of this debate—about the true meaning of customer-centricity—you and your colleagues would be unwittingly working at cross-purposes.

The power of the Miracle Question is in the way it sharpens and narrows your view of success. *A miracle has happened, and your marriage is fixed: How do you know it? Because your wife looked up from her book when you walked in.*

Notice that this is essentially the reciprocal of the "goal of the goal" question, which compels us to broaden out—starting with a goal and then widening the view to ask what its true intent was.

"What's the goal of the goal?" helps us see the destination and why it's important. (A Leverage Point must be something *worth doing*.)

The Miracle Question helps us identify the first productive

steps toward that destination. (A Leverage Point must be something *doable*.)

Broaden and narrow. The two prompts together serve as a clarifying tandem, a yin and yang of finding our way.

4.

Picking the wrong boulder—and thus the wrong Leverage Points—is a recipe for failure. I spoke with one CEO who said that, in each of the last three companies he had run, he had started by getting the teams focused on the right boulder. (Interestingly, in all three cases, the team's previous focus had been on something "extra"—ancillary businesses or acquisitions—and this CEO led them to refocus on the health of the core business.)

Achieving clarity on the way forward is not an incremental victory. It is transformative. It can mean the difference between stuck and unstuck.

A group of federal government leaders experienced this transformation several years ago when they rethought the goal of a program that served people with disabilities, including veterans. Some context: Anyone with a "total permanent disability" (TPD) can, by law, have their federal student loans discharged. But thousands of veterans didn't take advantage of the program. This was a disappointment to many government leaders, whose goal was simple: Make it easy for veterans to apply for the benefits they deserve.

What was holding back participation in the program? To some extent it was knowledge: Many simply didn't realize they were eligible for forgiveness. Others got derailed by the cumbersome application process.

The stakes were high: Some of these borrowers were actually in default—potentially having their social-security-disability payments garnished to make loan payments. The government was reaching into their pockets to claim money for loans that they shouldn't have owed!

So what could be done? In 2016, a team at the Department of Education (ED) thought: *Rather than make the borrowers responsible for discovering this benefit, let's proactively tell them about it!*

They hatched a plan that led them to compare the databases at several agencies, including the ED and the Department of Veterans Affairs (VA). The ED database could tell you: Who has student loans? The VA database could tell you: Which veterans are permanently disabled? Anyone who matched both databases was eligible for a loan discharge.

By mid-2018, the VA and ED had identified around 50,000 veterans who qualified for forgiveness. (Thousands of them were in default on those loans-they-didn't-really-owe.) Letters were sent to all of them, informing them that they were eligible for forgiveness and specifying how to claim it. So far, so good.

Ah, but then came *another* problem. The notification sent to veterans came under the letterhead of a private organization: the student loan servicer. The letter directed people to file their applications at a URL called "disabilitydischarge.com." To some recipients, it smelled a little fishy. *Uh, why isn't this coming from the VA? Why isn't it a .gov address? Is this story going to end with someone absconding to Cabo San Lucas with the remainder of my checking account?*

As one government insider told me, "Veterans just wouldn't do it. They were scared. I mean, it was every red flag you could possibly imagine."

In this situation, how could you encourage veterans to file their applications for forgiveness? Well, maybe send a less suspicious letter. Or set up a .gov website. Maybe some tweaks would ease the veterans' concerns.

But in 2019, the agency leaders stopped trying to iterate a broken process and took a hard look at the goal of the goal.

What's our goal? To help veterans apply for the loan forgiveness they've earned.

And what's the goal of the goal? To improve their financial security.

What are alternate pathways for achieving that goal, other than having them apply for forgiveness? Um, well, why don't we forget about the whole application process? Why do they need to apply at all? We can figure out who they are! Let's tell them that we can just FORGIVE THEIR LOANS. And then after their "okay," we'll let them know it's done.*

"There was a recognition that the letters clearly weren't working and there was a big push to make this automatic," a senior official at the Department of Education said. "It would be good for the borrowers but it could also be good for us—it could save us the time of processing a bunch of applications, sending them back again if they need to be corrected. Could this be a win-win for everybody?"

It was a radically simple idea, but it was no easy feat to implement. Just getting permission from different government agencies to compare databases—essential for forgiving loans—required a blizzard of paperwork that had taken months and months to push through.

The ripple effects of this policy shift have been broad and profound: Tens of thousands of disabled veterans—many of whom, again, had been in "default"—had their financial lives transformed. One disabled navy veteran saw her loan balance go from over

---

*Why did they need an "okay" first? There was a tax issue in some states: Forgiven loans might be treated as income, meaning that the vet would get an income tax bill for the forgiven loan. That's why the loan couldn't be forgiven automatically.

$72,000 to . . . zero. "I felt immense relief," she told a reporter. "I mean, I cried about it. I ugly cried about it."

The program was so successful, in fact, that it has since been expanded to other situations where people have earned (but not claimed) loan forgiveness. And that's often the way Leverage Points are uncovered. Someone comes up with a better way of doing things, and you think, *Aha! I can do that, too!*

But, as we'll see next, it doesn't always have to be *someone else* whom you learn from. The secrets of success might be right there, in your own team, hidden in plain sight.

Whirlwind review: Chapter 2, Consider the Goal of the Goal

1. The second way to identify Leverage Points is to take a careful and even skeptical look at the goals you're pursuing.

2. Often organizations set numerical targets as goals. Yet you can succeed at hitting these targets while utterly failing at your mission.
   a. *The dealership attracted great scores for customer satisfaction—but only because they were browbeating customers into rating them highly, regardless of their actual experience!*

3. To avoid that misalignment of goals and mission, you need to ask: What's the goal of the goal? And are there alternate pathways that might get us there more easily or quickly than the original goal we'd selected?
   a. *Marisa Lavars, a mother struggling with health problems, had originally set her New Year's resolution to get fitter. But after pondering the goal of the goal, she saw clearly: She wanted to be able to engage with her kids more often and more playfully.*

4. You can achieve more clarity about the "goal of the goal" by asking the Miracle Question.
   a. *The Miracle Question, in short: "A miracle happened overnight that fixed your critical problem. What are the first things you notice, after you wake up, that reveal the miracle has happened?"*
   b. *The married couple Elaine and Felix used the Miracle Question to identify little things that could change: "She would look up from her book when I came home."*

5. "What's the goal of the goal?" helps you see the destination and why it's important. (A Leverage Point must be something worth doing.) The Miracle Question helps you identify the first productive steps toward that destination. (A Leverage Point must be something doable.)

6. Achieving clarity on where you're really headed can be transformative.
   a. *The Department of Education changed its strategy from "making it easier to apply for loan forgiveness" to proactively forgiving those loans. As a result, tens of thousands of people were helped.*

Recommendations (find live links at <u>danheath.com/reset-links</u>):

If you need help picking the right boulder—i.e., knowing what to focus on in your work—then I'd recommend the thoughtful and practical *Bulletproof Problem Solving* by Charles Conn and Robert McLean. Rory Sutherland offers an <u>insightful take</u> on potential solutions we overlook because we don't think deep enough about the psychological goals of what we're building. His Eurostar example, mentioned briefly in this chapter, comes around minute six. Linda Metcalf literally <u>wrote the book on the Miracle Question,</u> a step-by-step guide to seeing your way quickly through confounding situations to meaningful and lasting change. Its primary focus is on personal relationships, but it also includes some advice on how to build more effective connections within the workplace. If the truck-buying story inspired you to think more carefully about how to set the right goals, check out this <u>paper</u> called *Goals Gone Wild* (and an accompanying <u>Q & A</u>). When goals go wrong, they can go very wrong.

STUDY THE BRIGHT SPOTS

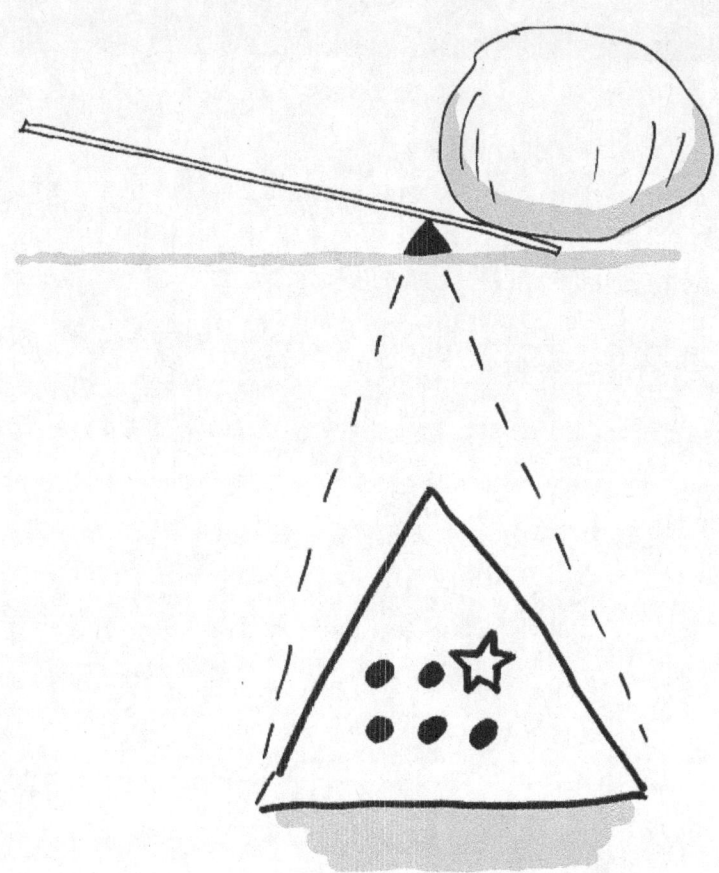

>> You can Find Leverage Points by
analyzing your own best work.

STUDY THE BRIGHT SPOTS

1.

In 1926, US military leaders were designing an airplane cockpit for the first time. The bodies of hundreds of pilots were tape-measured, and the average of those measurements informed designs for the size and shape of the seat and the height of the windshield.

For decades, that standard design endured. Then, in 1950, it was time for an update. Gilbert S. Daniels, a 23-year-old lieutenant, was part of the core redesign team. This time, the team measured over 4,000 pilots, studying 140 separate dimensions: Thumb length. Crotch height. Span from eye to ear.

The idea was that with more precise specifications, a more ergonomic cockpit could be created, which would lead to better pilot performance and fewer crashes. Or so it was thought. Daniels was skeptical. Were the "average" dimensions really the key consideration? How many pilots were average?

Daniels combed through the data. He analyzed 10 physical

dimensions in particular—including height and sleeve length—that were thought to be critical for designing cockpits. For each dimension, he computed the average. For height, it was 5'9". Then he broadened the average to include everyone who was in the middle 30% of the distribution. So, with height, the 30% middle range included all pilots between 5'7" and 5'11".

Daniels asked himself, how many pilots were in the middle range on *all 10 dimensions*?

Here's what Daniels found, according to Todd Rose, who tells the story in his fascinating book *The End of Average*:

> . . . even Daniels was stunned when he tabulated the actual number.
>
> Zero.
>
> Out of 4,063 pilots, not a single airman fit within the average range on all ten dimensions. One pilot might have a longer-than-average arm length, but a shorter-than-average leg length. Another pilot might have a big chest but small hips. Even more astonishing, Daniels discovered that if you picked out just *three* of the ten dimensions of size—say, neck circumference, thigh circumference, and wrist circumference—less than 3.5 percent of pilots would be average sized on all three dimensions. Daniels's findings were clear and incontrovertible. *There was no such thing as an average pilot.* If you've designed a cockpit to fit the average pilot, you've actually designed it to fit no one.

The air force's leaders, to their credit, took this finding seriously. They abandoned the idea of tailoring the cockpit to an "average pilot." Instead, they asked airplane manufacturers to create an adjustable environment, one that could accommodate pilots whose measurements spanned almost the full spectrum of possibilities: from the 5th to the 95th percentile on each dimension.

The manufacturers squawked. Such customization would be too expensive! Too slow! Eventually, though, they did what most business leaders do when confronted with losing gigantic customer orders: They caved. And they figured it out.

Suddenly, everything could be tweaked. Adjustable foot pedals. Adjustable seats. Adjustable helmet straps. All could be tailored to the individual pilot. As a result, pilot performance soared in the years afterward.

2.

Like the air force, you need to rebel against averages. Most leaders oversee their organizations using averages and aggregations: Revenue is an aggregation. Profit margin is an average. Net Promoter Score is an average.

Averages are great for monitoring but terrible for diagnosis. Averages can tell us: Something's wrong. But they're unlikely to tell us what's wrong, or how to fix it.

To Find a Leverage Point, we must push beyond averages. Disaggregate our rolled-up numbers. Disentangle the individual people and products and customers that together compose our organizations.

What we're looking for, in this chapter, is something very specific: Within the context of your goal, when have you been at your best? Let's call those unusually positive data points your "bright spots," a term my brother Chip and I used in our book *Switch*.* In the context of employee engagement, your bright spots would be your most engaged employees. In the context of corporate training, your bright spots would be the most effective or highly rated events. In the context of your own efforts to cut back on sweets, your bright spots would be the days you managed to avoid eating a brownie in the afternoon.

Bright spots make great Leverage Points because you know they're *possible*. If you've done something once, you can probably do it again.

But bright spots are typically buried in averages, so they are not self-evident. You've got to excavate them. That was Ken Davis's mission when, in 2009, he was asked to handle a crisis: a plunge in customer retention caused by the Great Recession. Davis worked at Gartner, the public research and consulting firm, and one of the company's key businesses involved selling market research subscriptions to corporate clients. In the aftermath of the economic crisis, as clients looked for places to trim expenses, costly research subscriptions looked like a tempting place to start.

For a subscription business, retention is the single most important measure of health. *Do your customers want to keep buying what you're selling?* And Gartner's customers were increasingly saying "no." By the middle of 2009, the wallet retention rate had dropped

---

*Switch focuses on behavior change, while this book is aimed more at the systems level (operations and strategy). But they're definitely birds of a feather! The most direct intersection between the two books is the focus on "bright spots." There's a full chapter on the topic in Switch, too, with all different material (don't miss the story of child malnutrition in Vietnam) and a greater emphasis on the psychology of why we obsess more about problems than about successes. If you like this book, you're likely to like Switch, too. And if you don't like it, it's definitely Chip's fault.

to about 84%. Meaning: For every $100 in subscriptions Gartner had sold in 2008, they were averaging $84 in 2009. Not good.

The people in charge of retention at Gartner were called "client partners," and Davis's first move, after taking over the group, was to *go and see the work*. As he learned more about the client partners and their work, he was struck by the disjunction between goals and activities. The #1 goal of the group was to maximize retention, yet much of their time was spent doing ancillary work: booking sales orders, collaborating with salespeople on selling new deals, and more.

"A big part of my initial work was 'clearing the decks' of all distractions," said Davis. "We needed to focus on the most important economic driver and literally drop everything else." (We'll return to this theme later in chapter 8, *Do less AND more*.)

In the next stage of his work, he dug into the data for clients who had renewed and clients who had churned. One insight came quickly: Those clients who regularly *used* their subscriptions were more likely to renew.

Obvious, perhaps. But the next insight was not so obvious, and it came from untangling averages.

Let's start with the graph below. The bar height represents the number of client partners who achieved different levels of retention.

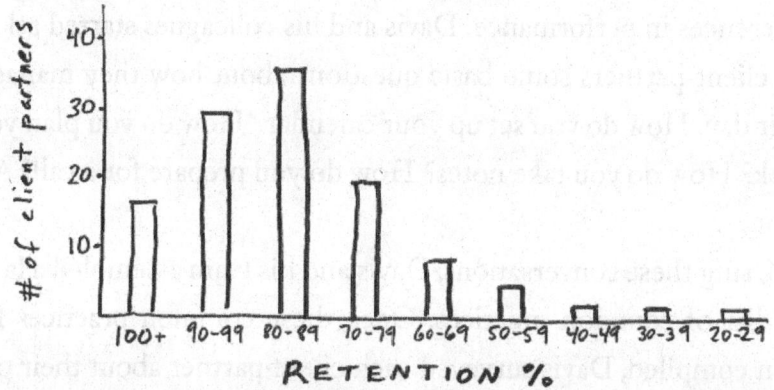

The vast majority of client partners (namely, everyone below 100%) were losing money, relative to the previous year.

Despite the (abundant) bad news contained in the chart, Davis's attention was drawn to the far left of the graph:

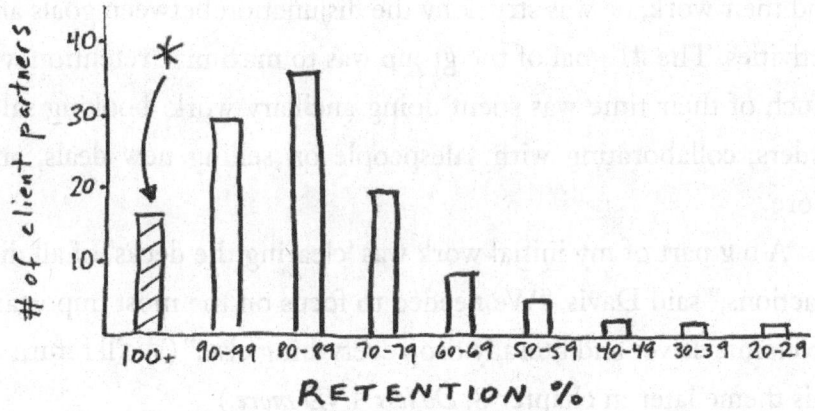

This was extraordinary: There were 17 client partners who had 100% or better wallet retention. (To go over 100% would mean that the accounts they managed spent more money this year than last year—a sign of a healthy business.) This was outstanding performance in the face of a recession. What were these high-performing client partners *doing* that was different from all the others?

Ken Davis launched a study of his team's bright spots. He believed that there must be differences in behavior underlying their differences in performance. Davis and his colleagues started asking the client partners some basic questions about how they managed their day: How do you set up your calendar? How do you plan your week? How do you take notes? How do you prepare for a call? And so on.

Using these conversations, Davis and his team assembled a laundry list of common practices. Once these common practices had been compiled, Davis surveyed each client partner about their own behavior. *Here's a list of practices that your colleagues use. Which ones do YOU use?*

Armed with those survey results, Davis was ready to answer the question: What are my A performers doing differently from my F performers? As an example, consider the practice of using a "follow-up process": getting back to clients with any resources or information that they requested on a call.

Here's the percentage of A and F performers who reported using that practice:

Follow-up process   73%   67%

What do these numbers tell us? In a nutshell: This ain't it. Using a follow-up process is not what distinguishes the top performers from the bottom, because both groups follow up in roughly equal numbers.

By contrast, check out this finding:

Defined daily process   87%   33%

That's a huge gap. Almost all the As used a "defined daily process" and only a third of the Fs did. And what is this mysterious "defined daily process"? It's basically thoughtful time management. One example from an A performer: "I reach out to 30–40 clients a week. I use Monday as a call-out day and prioritize my call-outs based on renewal dates."*

As a result of this bright-spots work, Davis unlocked the second big insight: Client partners had demonstrated radically different success rates at *getting their clients to use their subscriptions*, which was the single biggest factor in determining whether they ultimately renewed.

So a behavior like "defined daily process" (1) allowed the client partner to make more client calls, and those calls (2) encouraged clients to use their subscriptions more, which (3) boosted their odds of renewing. That was the logic of success.

In all, a set of nine specific behaviors seemed to separate the top performers from the worst. By *studying the bright spots*, Davis had uncovered a credible explanation for the difference in performance.

So his next move was to get his full team to push harder on those Leverage Points. The bright-spot partners trained the whole team on what they were doing. *Here's how I set up my calendar. Here's how I keep tabs on what my clients' business priorities are.*

As a result, the B, C, D, and F client partners started getting better. It wasn't mysterious what was driving better performance, it was an identifiable set of behaviors, and the client partners could practice and master them.

---

*Notice there's a natural link between finding bright spots and then going and seeing the work. You identify a bright spot in the data, then you go study it. The reason the latter is so important is that bright spots (in this case, great client partners) don't always know why they are bright spots. They're just doing what seems right to them (just as the underperformers are doing what seems right to them, too). It takes observation to identify the practices that are making them excel.

The results of this work were stunning. The year after the work began, Gartner had its best-ever level of retention.*

Then, in the second year, the retention number improved again. And again in the third year and the fourth. For 10 years in a row, the retention number kept hitting greater and greater highs.

Every year, they ran the same game plan: They studied the bright spots from the year prior, identified the key Leverage Points, and spread those practices to the full team. Davis's goal was for the whole team to achieve the level of performance that the bright spots had achieved the previous year.

A rough estimate is that Gartner's revenue increased by at least $100 million as a result of this relentless focus on untangling the averages. Pretty astonishing results from just studying your own people at their best.

3.

By studying bright spots, we can identify the circumstances that allow us to succeed. And if we understand those circumstances, we can replicate them, allowing our success to spread. You can analyze bright spots on any level: bright spots in your own life, bright spots in a team, bright spots among different departments in one

---

*The success was mostly but not *exclusively* due to the bright-spots work. For example, there was the matter of the extreme underperformers. Ken Davis's attitude was: If you're willing to learn, we want you on the team. But there were a few people who weren't willing to try. Davis recalled one woman who balked at the idea of trying to increase her number of client calls. She didn't think of herself as someone who served clients. She saw herself as more of a "strategic planner." As Davis told me, "If you want change you've either got to change the people . . . or change the people." The strategic-planner person had to find another job.

organization, or even bright spots across different organizations doing similar kinds of work.

Kate Hurley adopted that last approach in her quest to improve animal shelters. Hurley was a veterinarian and the first person in the world to do a residency in the new field of shelter medicine, which is devoted to studying shelters as a "system" with multiple goals: Keeping animals healthy. Reducing euthanasia. Ensuring the health of the animal population within the community.

In one of her first consulting assignments, Hurley and a fellow shelter-medicine expert named Julie Levy worked with the city shelter in Jacksonville, Florida. The shelter was dangerously overpopulated. Only 1 cat in 10 was leaving the shelter alive— the remainder were either euthanized or died from diseases that spread like wildfire through the overcrowded facility. "It was spiraling downward," said the shelter director, Ebenezer Gujjarlapudi. "We were running out of room. There was disease and rats. We were having to kill a lot of small kittens because they were getting sick."

The shelter workers were unhappy, ground down by the relentless cycle of euthanasia. Keep in mind: These are animal people! In a cruel irony, their jobs demanded that they put down animals. "You start getting angry," Gujjarlapudi said. "Or you begin to lose hope."

Hurley empathized with them: In her days as an animal control officer, she'd had to handle the euthanasia, too. It was one of the experiences that had sparked her interest in shelter medicine— reassessing shelters from a systems perspective.

In the midst of this Jacksonville dystopia emerged an idea so big and so effective that it would come to transform the world of shelters. The idea came from Gujjarlapudi, the person who had hired Hurley and Levy to consult. He was actually new to shelters: As head of another city department, he'd recently been tasked with overseeing animal care and control in Jacksonville. He didn't know what he didn't know. But that ignorance would turn out to be genius.

To understand his idea, we first have to understand the practice of TNR: trap, neuter, return. As Hurley explained, "So that's where you've got some cats living in your alley. You don't want them having a million babies. You don't want the males yelling and pissing on your car. In most communities, there's a TNR clinic where you can trap the cat and then bring it to a clinic. We spay it or neuter it, vaccinate it for rabies and other cat infections, and cut the tip off its ear so other veterinarians will know it's been done. Then we just put it back." In most communities TNR was handled by clinics and not by the shelters, whose goal was to find new homes for the cats through adoption.

So let's get back to Gujjarlapudi, who was facing an overcrowded facility where 9 out of 10 incoming cats would end up dead. He saw that some of the cats coming into the shelter had clipped ears. When he brought this up with the TNR clinic, they explained what the clipped ears meant and asked whether they could take those cats back, thereby taking them off Gujjarlapudi's hands. They'd already released them once—might as well try it again.

Then Gujjarlapudi asked a fateful follow-up: *Would you also like to take some of these other cats who aren't ear-tipped? You could just do your TNR thing and release them, and that way they won't end up euthanized.*

The TNR clinic said, *Sure, we'll take 'em.*

This was the heretical moment. Because shelters did not "return" cats to the community. They held cats in hopes of finding them a warm, adoptive family. That was the fantasy, at least. The reality was that many, if not most, shelters were so overcrowded that most cats had no hope of being adopted. What if, instead, the cats were just treated and put back into the community?

Because not all cats were house pets. Many were feral. Others were "neighborhood cats," living outside and making a daily circuit among many different homes. They didn't need adoptive homes to survive! They were doing fine on their own. Maybe all they needed was to be vaccinated and sterilized—and then released.

Hurley realized immediately the near-magical power of the solution. "It was a total holy sh** moment," she said. "It was just in a flash that I saw: Oh, this entire system that we've been burdened by for 100 years—it was built on a fundamental premise that was never questioned until this guy who didn't know any better asked, 'Could you just put them back?'"

"Return to field"—the name for what Gujjarlapudi had proposed—addressed so many problems at once. Once sterilized, the cats wouldn't contribute to overpopulation. Once vaccinated, they wouldn't spread disease. Once released from the shelter, they wouldn't clog up space and staff time, meaning that the remaining cats were healthier and better cared for and more likely to be adopted.

The shelter staffers were thrilled because they spent less time euthanizing cats and more time placing animals with families. "The staff now had a little breathing room," Gujjarlapudi said. "They're thinking, *Wow, what else can we do?*"

Best of all, those cats who weren't likely candidates for adoption—the ones who would have ended up euthanized—*got to keep living*.

The obvious objection to this approach—expressed by many animal control officers—was, *Wait just a darn minute—the community is going to be overrun by cats!* Hundreds of cats that previously were being caged or euthanized would now be set free. It would be pandemonium.

But it didn't happen. According to Hurley, one reason was that spaying and neutering changes the cats' behavior. "The cats just immediately become fat and lazy and calm themselves down," said Hurley. "They become better citizens of the community."* So even if there were more cats around, they were cool cats. Not trouble-makers.

Another factor at play here is more subtle (and fascinating): Could return to field actually *lower* the total population of cats?

That sounds absurd. How could you release more cats into a community and see the population numbers decline? It's like pour-ing water into a cup and seeing the volume of liquid decrease.

The answer, according to Hurley, relates to the "carrying ca-pacity" of the community. Think of carrying capacity like a food bank, the sum of all the food available to feed cats, ranging from mice and birds to bowls of kibbles left outside by animal lovers. That food bank is not infinite. It can support some finite number of animals.

What happens when a cat (from among that finite number) is caged or euthanized? It opens up a spot at the buffet. "If you took the cat away, but you left the food there, guaranteed there's some other cat there who's just going to have twice as much to eat," said Hurley. And then—this is the crucial part—those new diners at the buffet will have litters of kittens. "That's how litter-bearing mam-mals work—they have offspring in direct proportion to how much food is available."

But when the food bank is being gobbled up by spayed and neu-tered cats, it crowds out cats who otherwise might have had lit-ters. Consider what happened in San Jose, California, where the local shelter became the first to adopt return to field based on

_____

* I'm not sure whether I would have the same response.

Jacksonville's experience. The shelter returned about 10,000 cats to the field. Many skeptics feared an endless revolving door of cats coming in and out.

But, no, the rate of cats coming into the shelter went down by 30%.*

Hurley knew she'd found her Leverage Point: something doable and worth doing. Something capable of moving the boulder of mass euthanasia. And she had located that Leverage Point by scanning the environment for bright spots. Notice the pattern of thought:

What's the problem? Cats being killed in overcrowded shelters.

Where is that problem NOT happening? (I.e., what are the bright spots?) There's a bright spot in Jacksonville, where the shelter director embraced the idea of return to field.

Is that situation fundamentally different from other situations where it might be used? (In other words, is there a reason to think it would ONLY work in Jacksonville?) No, the dynamics in the Jacksonville shelter were familiar and widespread.

Okay then, let's replicate the bright spot!

---

*By the way, I want to acknowledge that TNR has become controversial in the birder community because cats eat birds. That part, at least, is indisputable. So people who love birds say, "You're releasing more cats—that's necessarily gonna mean more birds die." Hurley's counterargument (as you read above) is that return to field shrinks the cat population. The birders don't buy that argument: "Cats are a highly destructive invasive species that should not be allowed to live outdoors at all" was the stance articulated in one *New York Times* article. It's all complicated and mostly I want to stay out of this debate because I'm a dog person.

Hurley shared her findings with a group of shelter leaders in Northern California. Everyone in the room shared the goal of saving cats' lives. So Hurley laid out five strategies for accomplishing that goal, a key one being "return to field." But she wasn't satisfied just giving a presentation. She wanted a commitment to do something.

She pulled out a yellow legal pad and challenged the attendees to write down three bits of information: Their name. Their shelter. And the number of cats' lives that they would save, in the next six months, by adopting the bright-spot practices she'd identified. When Hurley tallied up the number, she found the group had committed to save over 1,300 cats.

The new practices were more successful than the shelter leaders had anticipated. One group, which had pledged to save the lives of 15 cats, found that after a year it had saved 900. Hurley realized she needed to think bigger.

By late 2014, Hurley and her partner Levy were ready to unveil the Million Cat Challenge, an effort to scale the lifesaving practices to shelters across the United States. The Challenge aimed to save a million cats by the end of 2019.

Not ambitious enough, as it turned out. The network of cat champions exceeded this goal easily. They had saved 1.1 million cats *one full year* ahead of schedule.

By spring 2024, the number had rocketed up above 5 million cats. The campaign had been propelled by a bright spot that emerged almost by accident. It had been an idea from a new shelter director who didn't know enough to know that he shouldn't be suggesting it. An idea that ended up revolutionizing the field. That's the power of a well-chosen Leverage Point.

In 2019, Hurley got an email from a shelter director who had joined the campaign. The email said, "We've run into a problem we've never had before . . . Our shelter has 49 full bottles of Fatal-Plus which haven't been used and are at the end of their expiration date. How great is that problem to have?!"

Fatal-Plus is the trade name for the euthanasia solution used in shelters.

It wasn't needed anymore.

Whirlwind review: Chapter 3, Study the Bright Spots

1. The third way to identify Leverage Points is to study the bright spots—your most successful efforts. If you analyze what allowed you to succeed in those occasions, you can scale that success.

2. Averages are great for simple monitoring but terrible for diagnosis. If you want to spot Leverage Points, you must untangle averages.
   a. *The air force found that there was no such thing as an "average pilot." They needed cockpits that could be tailored to individual differences.*

3. Often the way to unlock forward progress is to analyze your own best people or projects or performance.
   a. *At Gartner, Ken Davis was facing a sharp drop in client retention. Rather than agonizing about what wasn't working, he studied his bright-spot client partners.*
   b. *Davis was able to isolate specific practices they used, such as a "defined daily process." Those practices were Leverage Points, and he could direct his whole team toward them.*

4. You can analyze bright spots on any level: bright spots in your own life, bright spots in a team, bright spots among different departments in one organization, or even bright spots across different organizations doing similar kinds of work.
   a. *Kate Hurley, in consulting with animal shelters, discovered a bright spot: the notion of "return to field." It became a critical Leverage Point in saving the lives of millions of cats.*

5. Finding Leverage Points can be a needle-in-a-haystack hunt. Some Leverage Points might seem promising but prove impossible. But bright spots are different—you know you can succeed, because you already have. (Can you do it more?)

Recommendations (find live links at <u>danheath.com/reset-links</u>):

I learned about the US Air Force's cockpit study from Todd Rose's fascinating book _The End of Average_. Rose, who headed the Mind, Brain, and Education program at Harvard, breaks down the myth of measuring individuals against the average in schools and at work. He's really good at showing how there are usually multiple pathways to success: the three approaches children take when learning to read, the seven distinct routes to career success, and others. For a more psychological take on change, including a closer look at the power of bright-spots thinking, check out _Switch_, by my brother Chip and me. For even more on bright spots—especially for social-sector work—see _The Power of Positive Deviance_ by Richard Pascale, Jerry Sternin, and Monique Sternin. ("Positive deviance" = bright-spots thinking.) If you're a cat person—or simply interested in learning more about how a pair of vets managed to save millions of cats—check out the _Unleashing Social Change podcast episode_ with Kate Hurley as a guest. For a master class on how Hurley approached fixes for overcrowding in shelters, watch her <u>virtual lecture</u> hosted by the San Diego Humane Society. Or, to learn more about the five lifesaving strategies used in the Million Cat Challenge, check out the <u>resources section </u>of the campaign's website. (As a teaser, one strategy was "managed admission," which was basically a way of relieving bottlenecks, a topic we will explore in the next chapter.)

TARGET THE CONSTRAINT

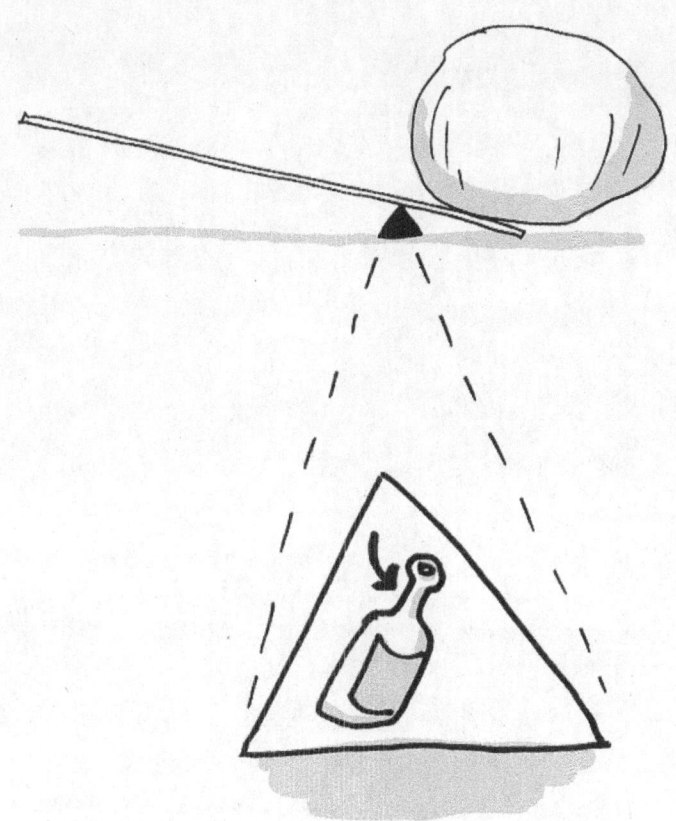

>> You can Find Leverage Points by assessing
the #1 force that is holding you back.

TARGET THE CONSTRAINT

1.

One night during the pandemic, I was sent to Chick-fil-A to grab dinner for the family. What I saw when I arrived was deflating: a seemingly endless line of cars for the drive-thru, snaking chaotically through the parking lot and twisting out onto the road.

I panicked. I hate lines. This was a half-hour wait, minimum.

I started fabricating wife-worthy excuses in my head: *Oh, sorry, honey, there was a road closed. So naturally I left the car and jogged the rest of the way, but it turns out they'd run out of chicken! Let's order pizza?*

Then I rallied myself. *No, come on, buck up,* I thought. I stared at the 50ish cars ahead of me. *Be a good dad.*

After one final moment of desperate mental bargaining—*What if I just offered my daughters extra screen time in lieu of dinner?*—I accepted my fate.

I rolled forward and entered the line.

Later I found that my experience was borne out in cold, hard data. *QSR* magazine published in 2023 a scorecard of how long it took, on average, for customers to get through a drive-thru line at 10 major franchises. Check out where Chick-fil-A landed:

CHAIN	TOTAL SECONDS REQUIRED TO GET THROUGH THE DRIVE-THRU
Taco Bell	279
Carl's Jr.	304
KFC	304
Arby's	320
Dunkin'	321
Hardee's	336
Wendy's	343
Burger King	351
McDonald's	413
Chick-fil-A	436

Dead last! You'd get through the line at Taco Bell about 2.5 minutes faster.

But let's get back to my predicament. Once I joined the line, something happened that tragically interrupted my sulking: I noticed that the line was moving. Almost constantly. It crept forward, steadily, like an automatic car wash.

I flipped from irritated to fascinated. This was the most operationally sophisticated drive-thru I'd ever seen. It ran like clockwork. (Cluckwork?)* By the time I emerged from the line, nuggets in the passenger seat, I promised myself I'd investigate the story.

It had taken less than 10 minutes to get 50 cars through the line.

This aspect of my experience, too, was reflected in a chart

---

*If you're viewing this as an ebook, there's an in-app purchase that allows you to remove all of these puns.

published by *QSR*. The previous chart showed the average time to get through the line. This one shows *the average number of cars in the line*. Note the Chick-fil-A number relative to its peers:

CHAIN	AVG # OF VEHICLES IN LINE
Chick-fil-A	3.40
McDonald's	2.00
Wendy's	1.50
Taco Bell	0.96
Burger King	0.92
Dunkin'	0.78
KFC	0.72
Arby's	0.67
Hardee's	0.48
Carl's Jr.	0.46

So the data is saying, yes, it's taking a while to get through the line at Chick-fil-A, but that's because there are a bunch of cars in line. The chain's speed, in terms of cars served per hour, is actually the best in the country.

And, as it turns out, my local Chick-fil-A (Roxboro Road in Durham, North Carolina) is one of the top five highest-performing drive-thrus in the entire chain. At its best, it has served 400 cars in an hour. That's a car every nine seconds. Your kids could get through college before Hardee's would finish 400 cars.

My local nugget source is basically the Usain Bolt of drive-thrus.

But it wasn't always that way. In the beginning, it was a normal Chick-fil-A with a normal drive-thru. Then, it made a series of critical changes over the years, one after another, that led to the present-day results.

Those changes were guided by a simple idea—one that you can use to boost your own change efforts. It's the idea of *targeting the constraint*, and it's the fourth of five methods you can use to identify Leverage Points.

What's the "constraint"? It's the limiting factor. It's the #1 force that is holding you back from doing your work better or on a greater scale. (I'm using "constraint" as a synonym for "bottleneck"—the two terms are similar, but I like the former because it seems broader and lacks the factory/operations connotations of "bottleneck.")* And in your search for Leverage Points, you are looking for candidates that *target the constraint*—that erode the obstacles standing in the way.

Chick-fil-A's steady progress over the years was fueled by continuous attention to constraints. "Drive-thru is all about flow," said Tony Fernandez, the owner/operator of the Chick-fil-A at Roxboro Road. "It's about managing the bottlenecks."

A key early Leverage Point was the embrace of "face-to-face ordering." Meaning that in the drive-thru lanes outside the restaurant, a human being stands next to your car and takes your order. It was a triple win: First, it's faster. The traditional menu board dazzles and delays customers. But with somebody standing at your window, you make quicker decisions.

Second, pushing the order takers upstream into the parking lot increased the amount of time the kitchen had to produce the meals, thus increasing the odds your food would be ready right when your car arrived at the window.†

---

*For readers intrigued by the notion of constraints, there's a classic business book you should immediately order called *The Goal* by Eliyahu Goldratt and Jeff Cox. It explains the "Theory of Constraints" via a fictionalized account of a failing factory and a failing marriage. It's an odd and compelling book and there's a reason it has sold more than 10 million copies.

†Weirdly, in drive-thru lingo, they call the window (where you get your food) the "door." I refuse to be complicit in this usage.

Third, and perhaps most important, untethering the operations from the menu board allowed Chick-fil-A to *scale*. A typical fast-food franchise might be stuck with one menu board (or maybe two if it's busy). But there's no natural limit on parking-lot attendants. In 2024, my Chick-fil-A would routinely have four or five people taking orders simultaneously.

In the early days, before tablet computers became common-place, the parking-lot attendants would call in orders to the kitchen via cell phones. Then, the constraint shifted to the checkout process, so they wheeled out the cash register to the parking lot using a superlong cable. As technology advanced, eventually the order takers could accept payment, too. Wireless tablets made it easy.

Periodically, the bottleneck would shift to the kitchen team (who make the food) or to "meal assembly" (the team who bundle and bag your order). More staffers would be brought on duty to relieve the constraint.

One day, one of Fernandez's lieutenants, Jacob Franks (and Jacob's brother Austin), flew a drone above the franchise to watch the line. (*Go and see the work.*) Watching the video footage, they noticed that when the line spilled out onto the street, cars tended to abandon it. I could relate.

That insight sparked an idea for another Leverage Point called "closing the gaps," which meant that while your order was being taken, you were encouraged to keep your car creeping forward, with the order taker walking alongside you as you discussed nuggets and sauces. That forward movement let them shrink the space between cars, which accommodated more cars in the lot, which reduced the chance that the line would overflow onto the street, which prevented potential customers from bailing.

Closing the gaps had a psychological payoff as compelling as the operational one. Fernandez and his team learned that what drove customer satisfaction was *not necessarily* minimizing the wait time. It was the feeling of progress. That steadily creeping 50-car line at Chick-fil-A, which takes seven minutes to complete, is actually preferable to idling in the five-minute line behind two cars at Taco Bell. It's less painful. (Uncanny, isn't it, how this mirrors the progress principle from the introduction? The feeling of progress is psychologically precious.)

Keep in mind that, even as you improve your operations, the constraint never goes away. As one area gets better, the constraint shifts elsewhere. When I first met Fernandez, the active constraint in the system was the "beverage cockpit." The laws of physics would simply not allow the team to pour the drinks into the cups quickly enough to keep up with the line. They needed more drink dispensers, but there wasn't room, so they had to wait for an expensive renovation that more than doubled the capacity of the beverage cockpit.

By mid-2024, the constraint was back to meal assembly. They're working on it. The new goal was an unprecedented 500-car hour.

Fernandez joked that, someday, he'll hire quarterbacks to work the drive-thru window, so cars can just roll by without stopping, their food thrown through the window in a perfect spiral.

2.

What's counterintuitive about constraints is that even smart-seeming investments can be worthless at improving the operations of a system if they don't address the constraint.

Here's a simple example. Let's say you're running a donut stand at a county fair. One person cooks the donuts, which takes 60 seconds, and the other person takes the orders, which takes 90 seconds. The stand is busy all day, with a long line of customers waiting.

Imagine that a salesman approaches you after hours with a special donut fryer that will cut your cook time in half, from 60 seconds to 30 seconds. It's expensive, but that's a huge improvement! The fryer is a solid Leverage Point—you should buy it, right?

No. Because if you think of the overall system, you're working on a rhythm of 90 seconds per customer. Every 90 seconds, a happy customer walks away with donuts. And the "gate" on your system performance—the bottleneck—is the ordering process.

So if you could cook donuts in 30 seconds instead of 60, the system as a whole wouldn't get any faster! Not one second. You wouldn't serve any more customers. Your cook would just have a minute of idle time in between every customer checkout. So the fancy fryer is not a Leverage Point because it will not speed up your operations.

To fight the constraint, you should hire another order taker. With two order takers going, you'll be checking out one customer on average every 45 seconds, which means that now the constraint flips to the donut-cooking (which takes 60).

So NOW it's time to call the donut-fryer salesman. Buy it. That lets you cook donuts every 30 seconds, which means the constraint flips back to ordering. If you hire a third order taker—three people taking orders at 90 seconds apiece means a system average of 30 seconds—then, presto, you've got a lightning-fast system that's harmonized at 30 seconds per order. You've tripled your speed.*

You could theoretically keep running this game plan forever, whittling the time down, down, down. But eventually you'll run out of customers. You'll have a small army of bored staffers sitting around, checking their phones. The constraint flips to marketing.

---

*Have I created this whole thought experiment about donuts so that my visits to Krispy Kreme will be tax-deductible? Perhaps. Might save me some dough.

So, in the world of operations, the notion of a constraint is rigid. Mathematical. In other contexts, the constraint may be less scientific. But it's still relevant.

Let's zoom far away from fast food. Away from scale, away from speed. Let's consider the home-care business, in which customers hire caregivers to attend to their (in most cases) very old relatives. The caregivers are not trained medical personnel; rather, they help with the daily activities of life: bathing, shopping, cleaning, cooking. They also provide companionship. Often, the people they care for live alone.

So this is a business that's personal, complicated, human, compassionate, messy, difficult. The antifactory. But it still has a constraint! In the post-pandemic era, the constraint on the growth of most home-care businesses was labor: finding and keeping good people.

It's hard to attract good people when the job demands intense, taxing work but the pay is close to minimum wage. Home-care leaders *could* pay their staffers a generous wage—say, $30 an hour! But then most of their business would evaporate, because their customers are regular folks paying out of pocket for their own relatives to receive care. For most non-rich people, it's a massive financial burden. There's just not much room to budge on wages.

So how do you hire extremely capable and dependable people for a subpar wage? Mostly, you don't. Workers cycle in and out of home care constantly. The median turnover rate in the industry is about 65%, meaning that two out of every three workers are gone within a year. Churn rates above 100% are not uncommon.

So that's your constraint. You can't grow because it's really hard to find more staffers who will work (reliably) at the wages you can afford to pay.

Laura Shaw-deBruin, the executive director of Norwood Seniors

Network, decided to aim her efforts squarely at that constraint. She was appalled by the high-churn norms of the industry. "It was embarrassing. It was not efficient," she said. "I wanted people to like where they worked. I wanted them to be happy."

To escape the endless churn cycle, she made two key changes: Norwood got pickier about whom it hired, and it fought harder to keep those chosen few. That required a substantial up-front investment—building a pipeline of candidates and constructing a set of filters to identify the absolute best employees. Each filter—detailed questionnaires, structured interviews, background screenings, a rigorous preorientation process—involves a meaningful drop-off rate.

The interview, for instance, is designed to weed out people who had the wrong instincts for home-care work. "It's amazing what people will say," said Shaw-deBruin. One scenario she offers sometimes is, *Imagine that you're working with an older woman who has dementia and she's getting angry at you and yelling. What would you do?*

Some candidates, Shaw-deBruin said, will say, *Well, I'd walk right out the door.* "When you're caring for somebody, you can't just walk out the door," she said. Some candidates have shown up for Zoom interviews while driving their car. One person logged in while taking a bath. (These people were not hired.)

The preorientation process, too, is burdensome, involving a physical and a drug test, among other steps. All of which must be delivered on a strict deadline. "If they're late on things like that, we don't even bother hiring them," said Shaw-deBruin. "If they can't get the things done on time, are they not going to show up to a shift? We value reliability."

Only 3% or so of Norwood's applicants are hired. They're the cream of the crop and are often caregivers at heart. Once hired, Norwood wants to keep them.

The firm tries to carefully match caregivers with clients, but the caregiver has a veto if the fit doesn't seem right. The match is critical, since the relationships can last for years. "We have a client right now who smokes weed and drinks all day," said Shaw-deBruin. "That's all he does. He's retired and this is how he wants to spend his retirement. He is not aggressive. He's not hurtful or nasty. He just doesn't give a hoot about anything. But without us there, he won't eat or shower. So we help him, remind him to do those things. And we take him places because he does not get in the car anymore, thank goodness. One of the caregivers I have with him is just as old as he is . . . very laid-back. And they work perfectly together."

Norwood built a mentoring program that matches new hires with more experienced staffers. Home care can be "very isolating" for new workers, said Shaw-deBruin. "I wanted them to feel connected." Now, they're contacted by a peer on their first day. And then again on the 30-, 60-, and 90-day milestones. The program gives them someone to talk to—someone who's not a boss. Someone who can relate to the countless daily hardships of caregiving.

At Chick-fil-A, the constraint bobbed around—from ordering to payment to baggers to beverages and so on. As the constraint shifted, so did the Leverage Point—the part of the system where applying force could permit disproportionate progress.

At Norwood, by contrast, the constraint holds rock steady, and so does its strategy. The constraint is labor quality and retention—all day, every day. So the firm's leaders have identified Leverage Points to relieve that constraint: a tough hiring process and a mentorship program and careful attention to matching the right caregiver with the right client.

All this attention to retention has paid off: Caregivers stay with them. Norwood is now consistently below 30% churn, which is rare in the industry. And it's no mystery why the firm has had that success: *It thoughtfully and consistently applied resources to relieving the constraint.*

3.

Constraints are contingent on a goal. If you were to ask, "What's the constraint at my kid's school?" that question doesn't compute. Constraint on *what*? The constraint on *smaller class sizes* might be a lack of teachers. Or classroom space. The constraint on *improving the student experience* might be the lack of interactive lessons in classrooms (reminiscent of the "shadow a student" story in chapter 1).

Chick-fil-A found its constraint in the context of *improving the flow of its drive-thru*. Norwood found its constraint in the context of *growing the business*. How do you find the constraint for the goal you've identified?

Often the "go and see the work" advice from chapter 1 will do the trick. When you observe how the work happens, you'll naturally spot blockages. Where are there pileups or delays?

Or try asking yourself this question: If you were allowed to hire one person to help you achieve your goal, what would that person's role be? The role you identify might well be the epicenter of the constraint. Once you realize this, you might be able to mitigate the constraint even if you can't actually hire someone.

Even individuals have constraints. The couples therapist Laura Heck deals constantly with unhappy fighting couples, and it's her job to identify what's holding them back and find some way to reverse the bad feelings. What's something that's small enough for them to embrace immediately—but also big enough to matter? What could possibly serve as a Leverage Point in a failing marriage?

Heck frequently recommends to her clients an activity called "sticky-note appreciations." Here's how it works: You keep a sticky-note pad and a pen right by the toothbrush holder in the bathroom. Then, while you brush your teeth, you're thinking about something positive you noticed about your partner. Something you appreciated. You write it on a sticky note and leave it on the mirror for them to find: "Thanks for making time to talk college stuff with Lucas—you're so good with him."

"I'm hoping to create an attitude of gratitude in their relationship where they're creating this desire to look for the positives," said Heck. "What's going right in the relationship? What do you love and appreciate about your partner? Because whatever we look for, we're going to find."

This activity is a reliable client favorite. And it's easy to understand why: People love finding those notes of appreciation twice a day.

Except that Heck said that those little bursts of joy are not really the point. "It might feel really good to receive a sticky note from your partner, but that's not actually the purpose of this," she said. "The purpose is to create a habit of mind where you're scanning for the positives. And it gets easier with time. So the more you start to tune into *What do I appreciate? What do I admire? What do I respect?*, the easier it becomes."

This is ingenious. As a therapist, almost everything is out of your control: the couple's past, their personalities, their emotions, their jobs and finances and kids. Not to mention that you might see them for only one hour in a week. The other 167 hours are out of your jurisdiction.

To repeat a riff from the introduction: When you're facing a big challenge, you can't change everything. You can't change *most* things. You can't even change a respectable fraction of things! But, with a bit of prodding and catalyzing, you can help change *something*.

For Heck, that *something* was to "create a habit of mind where you're scanning for the positives." That is a direct response to the key constraint in the couple's lives: the inability to see anything positive about their partners. They're not wearing rose-colored glasses, they're wearing jackass-colored glasses.

The sticky-note appreciations activity isn't a magic trick. It doesn't instantly solve a couple's problems. But it helps. It's a Leverage Point. For struggling couples who are hanging on to frayed hopes that it's possible to get back to where they once were, it's a chance to see the boulder budge.

4.

Because constraints make sense only in the context of goals, a logical corollary is that when you shift your goal, the constraint shifts too.

Think about the veterans loan-forgiveness example from chapter 2. In the beginning, when veterans had to apply for forgiveness, the constraint was "reducing the friction on applications." But then came the epiphany: *Hey, let's just proactively forgive those loans!*

That's a new goal. And as a result the constraint shifted to something more like: *getting permission from different government agencies to compare databases so that we can figure out whose loans should be forgiven.* Targeting *that* constraint, rather than the original one, makes a huge difference in how you direct your time and resources!

Similarly, with the Million Cat Challenge, the adoption of the "return to field" practice amounted to a brand-new goal for shelters. If your goal is to shelter cats in hopes of getting them adopted, and you're hopelessly overcrowded, your constraint might be the lack of space. Or the lack of families receptive to adoption. After committing to return to field, though, the constraint might shift to something more like: making sure there is enough surgical capacity to handle all the spaying and neutering that's necessary.

When you know where you're headed and understand what's keeping you from getting there, you can overcome that constraint and chart a better path forward.

Whirlwind review: Chapter 4, Target the Constraint

1. The fourth way to identify Leverage Points is to target the "constraint," or bottleneck—the #1 thing holding you back from your goal. Having identified the constraint, you can spot ideas for easing it.

   a. *At the Chick-fil-A on Roxboro Road, the drive-thru could serve a car every nine seconds! They achieved that level of performance by targeting the bottlenecks systematically.*

2. Constraints don't go away. When you relieve one constraint, you improve the system AND another constraint takes its place. There's always a constraint.

3. Investments that aren't directed at the constraint might do nothing to improve the system as a whole.

   a. *In the donut shop example, buying a new fryer would let you cook donuts faster, but that wouldn't help anything because the constraint (at the beginning) was the ordering step.*

4. Constraints can be clear-cut in operations-intensive environments. But every organization faces constraints, even if they aren't as simple to quantify.

   a. *In Norwood's home-care business, the constraint was finding trustworthy labor who would work for the wages the client could provide. To relieve that constraint, the firm hired more selectively and invested in retention and employee satisfaction.*

   b. *Even individuals have constraints. In Laura Heck's couples-therapy practice, the key constraint was "viewing your partner positively." So she prescribed the sticky-note appreciations activity.*

5. Constraints only make sense in the context of goals. If you shift the goal, the constraint will move, too.

   a. *In the Million Cat Challenge, shelters began to embrace the concept of "return to field." That, in turn, shifted the constraint to the availability of surgical capacity for spaying and neutering.*

6. When you understand deeply what is holding you back, you can spot possible Leverage Points that will allow you to shrink the obstacle and permit forward progress.

Recommendations (find live links at <u>danheath.com/reset-links</u>):

For more on the theory of constraints, I'm not sure whether anything can top the classic 1984 business book <u>The Goal</u> by Eliyahu Goldratt and Jeff Cox. It offers practical examples and lessons on how to evaluate an entire system (versus its individual components) as well as insights on organizational culture, leadership, and teamwork. And did I mention it's a novel? Also, 24 years after *The Goal*, Goldratt applied his philosophy of constraints to life more broadly through a conversation with his daughter, Efrat, in the book <u>The Choice</u>. For a practical, constraint-based approach to personal change, I'd recommend <u>How to Change</u> by Katy Milkman. She described her approach: "Change comes most readily when you understand what's standing between you and success and tailor your solution to that roadblock." If sticky-note appreciations struck a chord, you can hear more from Laura Heck on my podcast, <u>What It's Like to Be . . .</u> She gives us a peek into life as a couple's therapist—from the power of mystery dates to the rampant misuse of the word "narcissism." And finally, as a palate cleanser, enjoy <u>this comedic take</u> on what happens when "closing the gaps" at Chick-fil-A goes too far.

MAP THE SYSTEM

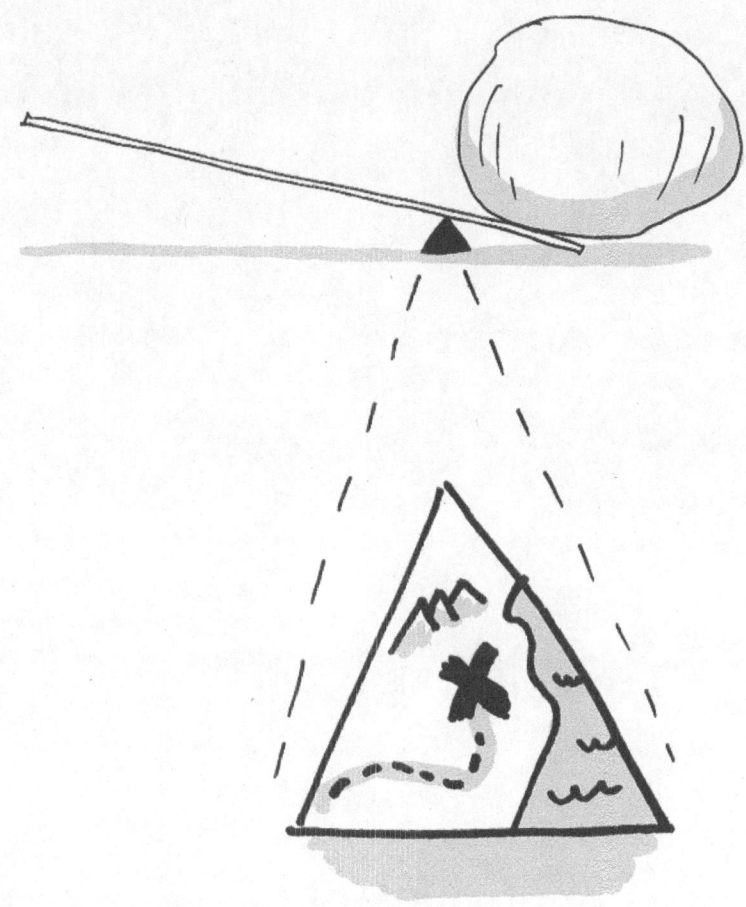

>> You can Find Leverage Points by rising above the silos to spot hidden levers.

MAP THE SYSTEM

1.

In 2018, two friends and colleagues, Geordie Brackin and Mike Goldstein, started questioning one of their longest-held beliefs.

The belief went like this: If students from low-income families could successfully graduate from college, then that degree would be their ticket to a financially secure future. Both friends had a stake in this belief: Brackin was a charter-school administrator, and Goldstein was the founder of a college prep charter school for low-income kids.

But both of them were starting to have doubts. "As I saw a lot of my students enter the workforce, I just started to get this creeping feeling that actually maybe the degree wasn't really helping them get jobs that were moving them out of poverty," said Brackin. "It wasn't the stuff of the American dream."

A Bain & Company analysis of college graduates from charter schools confirmed Brackin's intuition. Only half of those graduates were earning more than $40,000 per year, and 40% of them were holding jobs that did not require a bachelor's degree.

Goldstein said, "We started realizing, we've got a problem here because our whole theory of change is not what we had hoped." Brackin and Goldstein began to brainstorm about possible interventions that would help these students. *Their* students.

Freeze there for a moment. They were looking, in short, for a Leverage Point.

It was hard to conceive of a viable candidate, because the institutions and forces involved were so huge: families, schools, poverty, employers. A particular student might spend four years in a charter school, then four years in college, then start applying for jobs:

"Every system is perfectly designed to get the results it gets." So if the system depicted here was not delivering good jobs for graduating students, what could you potentially change?

Could you do something in high school? That would be an easy place to experiment for Brackin and Goldstein, since they were involved in charter high schools. But what kind of career prep, taught to a 16-year-old, would realistically arm them for success so many years later? ("Don't forget, six years from now, to write a really *personalized* cover letter . . .")

What about college? Maybe, but as a charter-school administrator, you have no control over college! It seems like a stretch to think you could influence the curriculum being taught.

What about the *career centers* in college, though? These groups exist for the sole purpose of helping college students get good jobs—a seemingly perfect spot for an intervention:

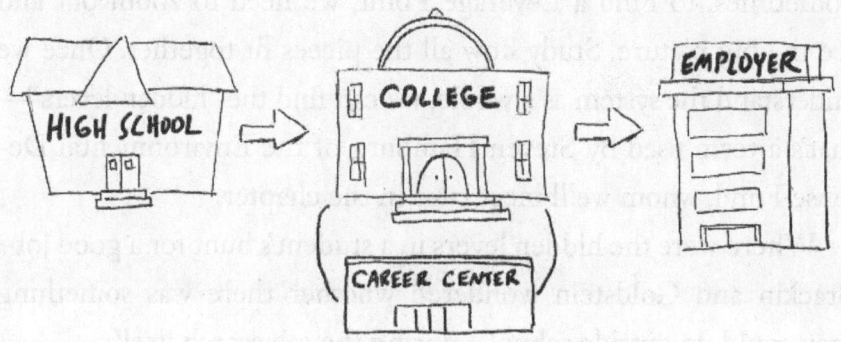

Intrigued, Brackin and Goldstein began to investigate how career centers operated. (*Go and see the work.*) What they learned was not encouraging. In summarizing what they had observed, Goldstein and Brackin channeled the voice of a fictional career counselor who had been freed to speak the hard, unfiltered truth to students:

> Our Career Office is not set up "to get you a job." We offer you mild edits on your resume, which helps your job search perhaps 3%. We give you a handout that tells you to "Network" but it's not obvious how to actually do this. We refer you to the Handshake online platform, which you will likely find frustrating to use. We may organize some career fairs, where you'll wander from table to table, confused about what to say or ask. Beyond that, we play dodgeball. You try to get our 1-1 help to make some introductions for you, genuine connections to real jobs, and we try to "dodge you" because we don't actually have many "connections" in that way. . . . We typically see any senior once or twice, then Bye.

By carefully analyzing the experience of students through schools and career centers, Brackin and Goldstein were *mapping the system*, which is the fifth and final way to identify a Leverage Point. Sometimes, to Find a Leverage Point, we need to zoom out and see the big picture. Study how all the pieces fit together. Once we understand the system as a whole, we can find the "hidden levers"— that's a term used by Steven Hamburg of the Environmental Defense Fund, whom we'll meet later in the chapter.

Where were the hidden levers in a student's hunt for a good job? Brackin and Goldstein wondered whether there was something they could do outside school—during the job search itself:

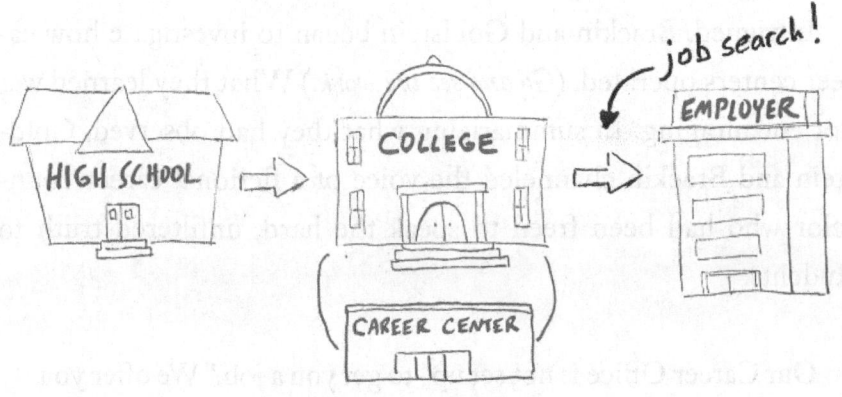

They zoomed in on that part of the map because both of them had been inspired by the success of "high-dosage" math tutoring, in which students received one-to-one instruction in courses where they were struggling. The intense, personal, highly customized approach often seemed to unlock success in a way that normal schooling could not.

They hatched the idea of high-dosage *career counseling*: an intensive period of coaching for young college graduates, with the goal of yielding a job paying at least $10,000 per year more than the graduates were currently making. They ballparked it as 30 hours of one-to-one coaching over a three-month period. It would be both a higher quantity and higher quality of assistance than students could get from any career office.

Brackin agreed to coach a few clients as an experiment—offering the help pro bono to lower the barrier for potential clients. He and Goldstein started looking for people who might be good candidates.

One of Brackin's first clients was Faith Carter. After college, Carter did administrative work for a title company, making $26,000 a year. Her mom had helped her get the job. Carter had applied for about 40 other jobs but received no callbacks.

She was an Ivy League graduate.

Another early client, Michael Deleon, worked for a nonprofit, and he was eager to find a role with more responsibility (and better pay). He had started applying for other jobs here and there, maybe once a month. But nothing ever landed—it was starting to get demoralizing.

It was Brackin's job to figure out why both of them were striking out. "The first order of business was like, 'Tell me exactly what you've been doing,'" Brackin said. "And the whole time I'm trying to diagnose where they've gone wrong or where they're stuck or where they've had this misconception about how the job search works."

Brackin found that Faith Carter had been applying for director-level positions that required years of experience that she didn't have. He helped her calibrate. With Deleon, interview practice was the key. "I used to speak a mile a minute in every conversation," Deleon said. "And so something I had to really practice was just slowing down. Also being more concise . . . I'm a good rambler."

For both of them, Brackin's guidance was a revelation, because they'd never received the feedback they needed to improve. "I was shooting all these shots into the air, but nothing was coming back," said Carter. "'No' is an answer, but nevertheless it still gives me nothing to work with. I don't know if they're declining me because I don't have enough experience, or I'm not the right fit, or whatever."

With Brackin's coaching, they started applying for the right jobs on a regular rhythm. A few months into their work, Deleon applied for a job as an assistant director of admissions at Haverford College. "I would've never even applied for this role if it wasn't for Geordie [Brackin]," he said. "No one's going to hire me to be an assistant director."

To his surprise, he was invited to interview. So Brackin arranged a series of mock interviews so Deleon could practice. When the day came to interview with Haverford, he was ready, and he endured the Zoom gauntlet of five successive interviews. He felt great about how he'd done.

But he didn't get the job. It was a tough blow to absorb.

Then, six weeks later, the dean of admissions reached out to him. The department had found the funds to create a new role specifically for him. "They connected to me through the interview process and they didn't want to lose me," said Deleon. "They wanted me on the team. . . . I was in shock."

He took the job. It paid $11,000 more than his prior role.

Meanwhile, Faith had applied for and landed a role at a private school that paid $20,000 more.

The high-dosage career counseling was working.

And it continued to work. All of Brackin's first 30 clients got a better job within a matter of months, with a median gain of $11,000 per year. Every single one.

"I think a key to Geordie [Brackin]'s success has been that people need somebody to untangle where they're stuck," said Goldstein.

"You find the 1 thing in 20 in a particular situation that's blocking them. And you can't do that with a formulaic response." (*Target the constraint.*)

With high-dosage career counseling, Brackin and Goldstein had found a viable Leverage Point—a 30-hour booster engine that yielded meaningful results. Before their efforts, it wasn't obvious to anyone that such a service could exist or that it could work. It was outside the scope of high schools. It was foreign to career centers. It was upstream of employers.

To find the Leverage Point, someone had to zoom out and *map the system*.

2.

The key move in *mapping the system* is to ascend above the silos: the individual units or departments within a larger organization (or across multiple organizations in the same field). Silos are the inevitable but regrettable consequence of a mission that's too big to conquer holistically. You can't run modern-day Microsoft out of a garage, informally, over pizza and beer. You must break it into 10,000 pieces, carved up by function and product and geography. Each team gains ownership of one piece of the puzzle. That's the only sane approach to managing a system with massive complexity.

Inevitably, though, team members start to worry more about their piece than the entire puzzle. The silo comes to overshadow the whole. Why? Because their work is in the silo. Their friends are in the silo. Their performance is measured within the silo, and their incentives are tied to the silo's results.

That's why *mapping the system* works best when it spans silos, because no one (other than the top executives of an organization) is paying attention to the whole. One tried-and-true method for transcending silos is to follow the path of a key customer or constituent: For, say, a software business, you might map the journey by which a customer discovers you, signs a contract, gets onboarded, and subsequently seeks support. ("Journey mapping" is a common term of art here.)

A team at the University of Iowa Hospital and Clinics (UIHC) mapped the flow of patients through the radiology department. The goal of the team's work was to eliminate the two-week wait time for patients to receive CT scans. For many of the people involved, it was the first time they'd been invited to see the big picture.

"In health care, sometimes people work in silos," said James Bahensky, one of the leaders of the improvement process at the clinic. "You've got the scanning activity, you've got X-ray activities, you've got other things, and they all work in their own separate areas. . . . They don't understand each other's processes."

The team traced the patients' experience from when they arrived at the clinic to when they left. When the team saw the whole, they noticed some obvious flaws. One involved "contrast" dye, the chalky solution that patients are asked to drink before receiving a CT scan. (The contrast shows up white on the scans, which can help the radiologist distinguish organs—and also spot problems.)

At UIHC, the first nurse who met with the patient supplied the contrast. After the patient guzzled it, things would come to a halt for an hour while the liquid made its way through the patient's GI tract. The team wondered: *Why are we waiting so long to start the clock on the contrast?* It was a costly delay.

The nurses had always been the ones to administer it, but, as Bahensky said, "nobody seemed to know why." It was just a drink. No real medical complexity involved.

So a few days into the sprint, they bought a refrigerator for the reception area, and now when patients checked in for a scan, the receptionist could just hand them a bottle of contrast. The time savings were huge—for patient and clinic alike—and it required . . . er, a new fridge.

This "buying a new fridge" type solution is exactly the kind of idea that will not emerge *within* silos. The receptionist can show up every day and manage his or her domain exquisitely—checking in patients efficiently and politely—but it will never once occur to them to say, "Hey, I should be the person administering contrast!" Nor will it occur to the nurses, "Hey, this medical-seeming thing I've been handling since time immemorial is probably best turfed to the receptionist!" Only with the systems-level view can you hope to unlock an improvement like this one.

During the sprint, the working team mapped not only the way patients flowed through the clinic but also their own movements within the space. They observed the clinic's technologists and created "spaghetti charts," which use noodle-ish lines to represent the movements of people over time. Here's a spaghetti chart for one particular tech:

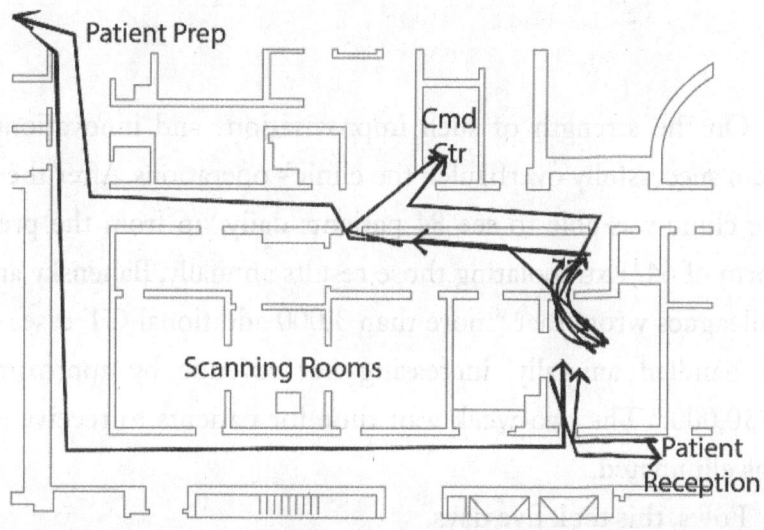

As you can see, there were some long walks involved: The technologist had been escorting patients from reception to the prep rooms. But from the systems view, it made more sense to let the tech stay focused on CT-scanning work. Someone else could do the chaperoning.

After the team redesigned the workflow, the technologist's new spaghetti chart looked like this—a 91% reduction in necessary steps. (We'll encounter more of this thinking about reducing waste ahead in chapter 7.)

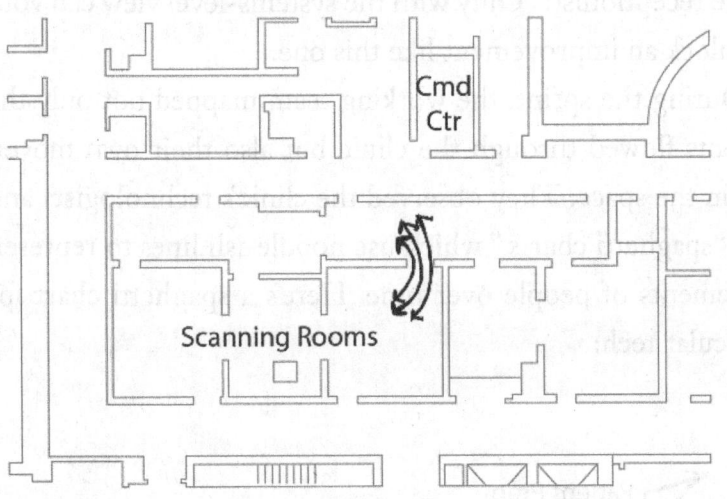

On the strength of such improvisations and innovations, the team successfully overhauled the clinic's operations. After the reset, the clinic was able to see 84 patients daily, up from the previous norm of 64. Extrapolating those results annually, Bahensky and his colleagues wrote that "more than 3,000 additional CT cases could be handled annually, increasing net revenue by approximately $750,000." The two-week wait time for patients to receive a scan was eliminated.

Folks, this took five days.

3.

The second crucial component of *mapping the system*—in addition to spanning silos—is challenging assumptions. As you come to understand how the different parts of a system interact, you'll need to start asking incisive questions: Why do we do it that way? Is there a better way?

Mike Goldstein and Geordie Brackin asked: What if we snapped some "high-dosage career tutoring" into the ecosystem? Would that burst of tailored assistance be enough to matter given the massive forces at play? Or recall that in the Million Cat Challenge story, a giant leap forward was triggered when the Jacksonville shelter director asked, *Hey, what if we just trap, neuter, and release some of these healthy cats that are in our overcrowded shelter?*

"The biggest challenge you have in thinking about systems is becoming aware of your assumptions, because the assumptions almost always drive how you view the system," said Steven Hamburg, the chief scientist at the Environmental Defense Fund (EDF).

We will close this section of the book by studying the work of Hamburg and his colleagues to Find a Leverage Point in perhaps the world's single most complex arena of action: the effort to slow down climate change. In previous chapters, we've explored how people found Leverage Points in small "systems" (a struggling married couple) and in larger ones (the effort to forgive loans for disabled veterans). Now, we'll see how the same logic applies even on a global scale.

One of Hamburg's early "assumption-questioning" moments involved, of all things, a van. As a professor at Brown University— his job before the EDF—he'd used a natural gas–powered van to shuttle his forest-ecology students to field sites every week. It was supposed to provide a cleaner, more efficient option than a gasoline-powered van. But did it, really?

Natural gas had been billed as the perfect fuel to "bridge" humanity as it transitioned from dirty energy (coal, oil) to clean energy (solar, wind). Natural gas burns significantly cleaner than coal and oil. But Hamburg didn't think it was so simple. Taking the van as an example: "We really didn't know if driving a natural-gas van was the environmentally better thing to do," said Hamburg. "None of the calculations included methane emissions." (Note: Methane makes up about 97% of natural gas, so many people use the terms interchangeably.)

Why weren't methane emissions taken more seriously? In the world of climate change, where scientists were constantly computing the effects of different changes on the environment, researchers had settled on the convention of computing things on a 100-year timeline. The convention was a compromise: A century was a long enough period to study the cumulative effects of carbon emissions but short enough that it stayed relevant to present-day leaders.

On this 100-year timeframe, methane didn't matter, because it was short-lived. Methane sticks around in the atmosphere only for about a decade; CO_2 can last for millennia. That's why CO_2 was the dominant (and often exclusive) focus of climate-change discussions, and why you hear about "carbon footprints" but never "methane footprints."

Hamburg realized that the assumption was problematic. Even though methane didn't *endure* for 100 years, that didn't mean it was irrelevant on a 100-year timeframe. Because during its short life, it packed a nasty punch. Because of its unique molecular structure, methane can trap up to 80 times more heat than other greenhouse gases, so even a small increase could have an outsized impact on how much the planet warms, and how quickly.

So, in a way, the natural-gas van became the perfect symbol of the folly of the timeframe assumption. Because when Hamburg did some basic math, he came to a startling conclusion: Yes, over a 100-year timeframe, driving a natural gas–powered van was better for the environment. But it was a net *negative* for the first 85 of those years! It turned positive *only during the last 15 years.*

So the van was bad for him. It was bad for his children. The van was bad for his children's children. But maybe one day his great-grandchildren could eke out some small benefit.*

Hamburg came to realize that the world was facing two climate crises—the carbon-dioxide problem (the dominant topic of discussion) and now a methane-emissions problem, too. You couldn't overlook either one. "We need to solve both," Hamburg realized. "It's not an *or*—it's an *and*." In *mapping the system*, Hamburg had discovered something unexpected and vital: "There was a hidden lever: reducing methane emissions—and doing it quickly and dramatically."

There are natural sources of methane emissions, such as wetlands. Those would be hard to contain. But other sources of emissions were preventable, such as leaks from the wells used to capture natural gas, as well as from the pipes used to transport it. To reduce methane emissions, those leaks would have to be located and plugged. That was no easy mission, though, since methane is odorless and colorless. (It's true that you can smell gas from your furnace or stove, but that's only because gas companies—for safety reasons—have added a chemical that smells like sulfur.)

With infrared cameras, though, leaks could be spotted. Once a leak was identified, fixing it wasn't rocket science, it was plumbing.

---

*To get real for a moment, though, your great-grandchildren are definitely not going to see a "benefit" to driving your hand-me-down 85-year-old van.

Better yet, for the energy companies involved, the leaks represented lost revenue—if natural gas escapes into the atmosphere, you can't sell it—which gave them a financial incentive (as well as a moral one) to take leaks seriously.

This financial incentive illustrates, once again, the importance of finding Leverage Points that are both *worth doing* and *doable*. It would be immensely valuable to our great-grandchildren's future if all current citizens would switch immediately to a vegan diet. That is *worth doing* from a climate-change perspective. But it's also very, very far from *doable*.

By contrast, reducing methane was both environmentally significant *and* of value to the exact industry doing the polluting.

At EDF, Hamburg and his colleagues—along with researchers from universities and the energy industry—expanded the hunt for leaks. What they learned, in some cases, was outright alarming: In the Permian Basin in West Texas, for example—the second-largest natural-gas area in the United States—methane was leaking at a rate 60% higher than the EPA's estimates. At that level of leaking, natural gas was worse for the planet than coal!

But Hamburg and his colleagues found bright spots, too. Early on, researchers scanned and inspected the Barnett natural-gas field in central Texas. One-third of the sites had either minuscule methane leaks or *none at all*. A buttoned-up system was possible, after all. (*Study the bright spots.*)

Even as the leak-chasers learned more and more about the system, their sense of dissatisfaction grew. "The studies give us snapshots but they don't give us the comprehensive view," Hamburg said. "They don't give us the movie. We've never had the data to answer three basic questions: Where are the emissions? How much are the emissions? And how are they changing over time?"

But answering these questions on a global level seemed a

far-fetched aspiration: Only an innovation worthy of science fiction could hope to provide that level of detail.

Then, the EDF team proceeded to cook up *an innovation worthy of science fiction*: They hatched a plan to launch a methane-tracking satellite into space. From orbit, using special cameras, the satellite could compile a real-time portrait of nearly every leak on the planet.

On March 4, 2024, that satellite—MethaneSAT—was launched aboard a SpaceX Falcon 9 rocket. It will provide real-time Leverage Points: Where are the biggest leaks? What would it take to plug them? Who has an incentive to do the plugging? It's an environmental dream.

The goal is to cut 45% of methane emissions within a few years, which is the carbon-footprint equivalent of shuttering one-third of all coal plants in the world. The satellite's price tag is $90 million. But if it can help to minimize the worst effects of the coming storms, fires, floods, and droughts, it will be a bargain. And a Leverage Point for the ages.

Whirlwind review: Chapter 5, Map the System

1. The fifth and final way to identify Leverage Points is to map the system—zoom out to see the big picture. You're hunting for the "hidden levers" in the system.

    a. *In trying to help low-income college graduates get better jobs, Mike Goldstein and Geordie Brackin saw that one promising place to intervene was during the job search itself (as opposed to during formal education).*

    b. *Their idea for "high-dosage career counseling" proved incredibly effective for all of their early clients.*

2. Mapping the system requires ascending above the silos both within and across organizations.

3. One reliable tool for mapping the system is to follow the journey of a customer (or patient or student) as they intersect different silos.

    a. *By following the patient journey through the radiology clinic, the clinic's staffers were able to spot valuable Leverage Points, such as having the receptionist administer contrast upon check-in.*

4. The second critical aspect of mapping the system, in addition to rising above silos, is the need to challenge assumptions.

    a. *According to EDF's Steven Hamburg, the assumptions always drive how you view the system.*

    b. *There was a key assumption that had deterred environmental leaders from focusing on methane: Because of its uniquely short life, it really didn't matter in the long run.*

    c. *By rethinking these assumptions, Hamburg and the EDF uncovered a "hidden lever" in the world of climate change: the opportunity to reduce methane emissions quickly.*

5. By studying the way systems function—and the relationships between their parts—you can Find Leverage Points that unlock progress, even on a global scale.

Recommendations (find live links at <u>danheath.com/reset-links</u>):

For more on Geordie Brackin and Mike Goldstein's deep dive into the failings of career centers—and potential Leverage Points for a way forward—check out their white paper, <u>*Peeling The "College Career Services Office" Onion*</u>. For a detailed, day-by-day account of how the University of Iowa Hospital's radiology department fixed patient wait times within a single week, here is its fascinating <u>case study</u>. For the director's-cut version of the methane story, read David W. Brown's *New Yorker* story "A Security Camera for the Planet." Also, be sure to watch Fred Krupp's inspiring <u>TED Talk</u> announcing the <u>MethaneSAT</u> project and its vast potential—around the 3:00 mark, he shows how infrared cameras can detect leaks that are otherwise invisible. There are methodologies for "mapping the system" that I felt were beyond the scope of this chapter, but I still think they are really valuable: (1) Journey mapping (mentioned briefly) is a good way to "map the system" for customers, patients, students, etc. For a primer on customer journey mapping, check out <u>Journey Mapping 101</u>. (2) Developing a "theory of change": <u>This guide</u> by Stanford's Center for Innovation coaches nonprofits through creating a theory of change for their efforts to change the world. It's about as comprehensive as you could hope for—complete with videos, exercises, and advice. (3) Drawing a "driver diagram": This is a really helpful visual tool for identifying the elements of a system that "drive" a certain outcome. More on those <u>here</u>.

SECTION 2

RESTACK RESOURCES

 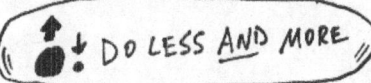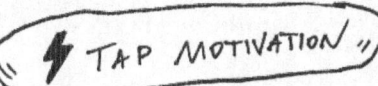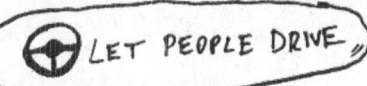

6

START WITH A BURST

>> You can Restack Resources on
your Leverage Points by beginning with
an intense and focused period of work.

START WITH A BURST

1.

"I was recently assigned the task—by a spouse who shall remain nameless—of installing a new hose system for the vegetable beds," wrote the attorney Greg McLawsen. "As any DIYer knows, there is an immutable law of the universe that one cannot acquire, in a single trip to Home Depot, all parts required for a project. It simply cannot be done. If you were assigned the task of replacing a single 60-watt light bulb, by the time you returned from Home Depot you would realize that a 61-watt bulb was actually needed, calling for a return trip to the store."

McLawsen went to Home Depot for his hose system supplies, and sure enough, the immutable law held true. One of the hose-splitters he'd bought had a leak, which rendered it useless. Until he could get a replacement, the hose system wouldn't work.

He realized that the efficient thing to do would be to wait for his next Home Depot trip—it would likely be within a few days, anyway—and add the hose-splitter to his shopping list, rather than make another special trip for one $2 part.

"But my wife didn't want me to be efficient, she wanted to be able to water the vegetables," wrote McLawsen. "My success or failure was judged by a single criterion—whether the vegetables could be gardened. Even though it was ludicrously inefficient, I got back into my truck and drove back to Home Depot, probably spending $3 of gas and $200 of my time in order to buy a $2 hose widget. Even though I did something inefficient to achieve my result, *I was effective because I got the project done.*"

McLawsen realized the lessons of his garden project also applied to his law firm: "The 10 LLC formation documents that you have 90% completed are currently worthless to you and to your client." Only 100% matters to the client.*

Sometimes it takes a flurry of focused efforts to accomplish something meaningful. It's like opening a window that's stuck—the force you need to *get it moving at all* can be dramatically higher than the force you need to *keep it moving up*. And that's where a burst comes in.

In the book so far, we've been searching for promising points of intervention. Where can you Find Leverage Points? Now that you've (hopefully) uncovered some candidates, we will shift our mission to Restacking Resources:

---

*On this theme of working to completion, a reader shared a great story about having a "Life Crap" month one July, which involved finishing many of adulthood's nagging tasks: revisiting a will, reviewing insurance policies, updating emergency contacts and account information, and many other boring but essential activities. Each one was pursued methodically until complete. The payoff? "Words are insufficient to express my satisfaction level on July 31."

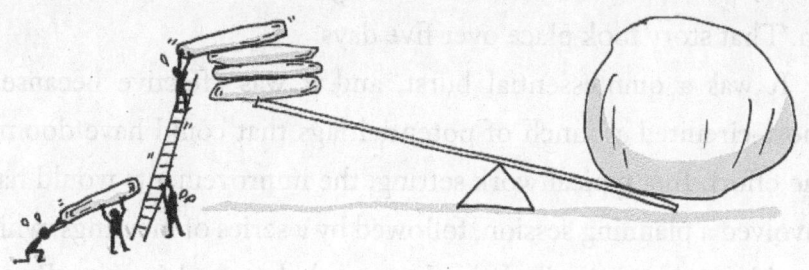

Because it's not enough to Find a Leverage Point. Having found it, you have to push. Where does the energy to push come from? It must come from within the set of resources you have at your disposal: money, labor hours, physical assets, data, and so on. But those resources, deployed exactly as they are today, are not yielding the results you want. That's why we have to restack them.*

In this section, we'll explore six different methods for Restacking Resources to push on your Leverage Point. The goal of all six methods—in visual terms—is to add weight to the business end of the lever shown above.

Our first method of Restacking Resources, the imperative to *start with a burst*, involves an intense period of work with single-minded focus on a goal. Recall the story of the radiology clinic from the previous chapter. The team made a series of big improvements: the receptionist would serve patients their contrast in the waiting

---

*By the way, if you have untapped funds, or if you can hire more people, or you can otherwise bring new assets to bear, then (of course) do that. I'm not going to focus on "adding more," since most people I encounter don't have that luxury. But if you do, then milk it! There's no shame in taking the easier route! You'll still follow exactly the same strategy laid out in this section—you'll still need to pay attention to waste, motivation, alignment, etc. You'll just have a little extra momentum thanks to those extra resources.

room, the workflow would be reconfigured to reduce steps, and so on. That story took place over five days.

It was a quintessential burst, and it was effective because it short-circuited a bunch of potential lags that could have doomed the effort. In a typical work setting, the improvements would have involved a planning session, followed by a series of meetings, which would spawn an email chain that spiraled toward infinity. But by using a burst, the colleagues could bypass all the bureaucracy and collaborate in real time.

A burst involves committing dedicated time to accomplish something meaningful. Greg McLawsen's gardening project was a burst—it got his exclusive focus until it was finished, even though working to completion required him to make that "inefficient" trip back to the store for a $2 part.

A burst is not about compelling people to work harder. It's not saying, "Hustle and work an extra 10 hours this week because we're in a burst!" It's saying, "Let's do this critical 40-hour project in one intact, focused week, because if we let it sprawl across six weeks, the 40-hour project will turn into a 115-hour project." It's about focus.

And this breed of focus has become an endangered species in our lives, for reasons we'll see next.

2.

Brigid Schulte was a self-proclaimed "hair-on-fire woman," struggling to balance her full-time job as a reporter with her obligations as a mother. In her book *Overwhelmed*, she wrote about visiting a social scientist whose research suggested that women like her should have 30 hours of leisure time in a given week. Schulte, understandably, found this claim rather incredible.

She said her life felt "scattered, fragmented, and exhausting." But she reluctantly agreed to keep a time diary, per the man's recommendation.

She faithfully logged her time in black notebooks. And she found that, yes, there were indeed many cumulative hours of "leisure." But the time didn't actually feel like leisure. It was more like a bunch of harried shards in between other activities. As she wrote:

> In tracking my time, I now know exactly how many minutes it can take to break your heart: seven. That's how long it took for my daughter to tell me, in angry tears as I finally cut her too-long fingernails in the bathroom one evening, that I was always at the computer and never spent enough time with her. And that, when she grew up, she wanted to be a teacher. "Because then at least I'll be able to spend time with my kids."
>
> In the conference room, hand still on my little black notebooks, I think of confetti. That's how my life feels. Like time confetti—one big, chaotic burst of exploding slivers, bits, and scraps. And really, what does a pile of confetti ever amount to?

"Time confetti": a brilliant phrase.

And we all know there's a work equivalent of time confetti. Our time is continuously carved up between meetings and emails and messaging and calls and to-do list items. A block of time for most workers doesn't look like this:

It looks more like this:

1 p.m. ☐☐☐☐☐☐☐☐☐☐☐ 2 p.m.
EMAIL   TEXTS   SLACK

Illustrations adapted from Ashley Whillans's *Time Smart* (HBR Press)

Every one of those seams in the bars you see above involves "task switching": the awkward transitions between activities, when your brain has to refocus and reorient. Task switching is one of those phenomena that have almost no redeeming features. Research shows that it makes us slower. Less effective. More prone to errors. More stressed.

Yet even as task switching shreds our momentum, we sometimes take a wrongheaded pride in it. *Look at how busy we are! We're such good multitaskers!* It can be self-perpetuating, too, because—as the psychologist Ashley Whillans points out in her book *Time Smart*, "When we feel time poor, we take on small, easy-to-complete tasks because they help us feel more control over our time."

Confetti begets confetti.

That's why bursts require a block of focused time. The excellent book *Sprint*—authored by Jake Knapp, John Zeratsky, and Braden Kowitz—provides a step-by-step recipe for staging a five-day design sprint. You convene a multidisciplinary team and you protect their focus. You give them the gift of unbroken time.

Knapp said a typical day for an employee looks like the picture below. The real work—the new priority you care about—gets squeezed in between a bunch of competing commitments:

But during a sprint, the core work dominates:

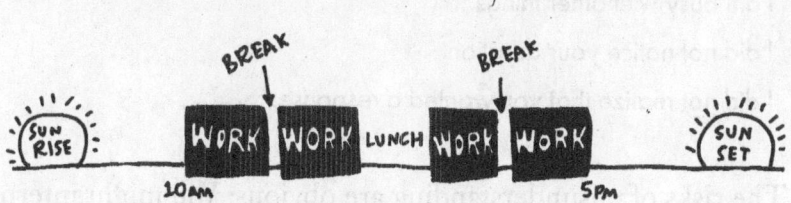

The work is the work. Everything else has to wait. And by the end of the week, the reward is that you have completed something: a mock-up or prototype.

Now, in a remote work world, this strategy gets more complicated. You can't get everyone in the same room (or at least not easily). And that remote collaboration can spark a variety of miscommunications and misunderstandings.

Catherine Durnell Cramton studied the way remote teams collaborated and she wrote, memorably, "One of the biggest challenges team members faced was interpreting the meaning of their partners' silence."

In other words, imagine that you sent an email out to several colleagues in different offices, expecting a reply from everyone. Some people replied and some didn't. So you're left wondering, about those who didn't reply, what does their silence mean?

Cramton found that, over the course of the project, "silence had meant all of the following at one time or another:

"I agree.

I strongly disagree.

I am indifferent.

I am out of town.

I am having technical problems.

I don't know how to address this sensitive issue.

I am busy with other things.

I did not notice your question.

I did not realize that you wanted a response."

The risks of misunderstanding are obvious: You might interpret someone's silence as "I strongly disagree"—and begin scheming against their unjust resistance—when they're simply out of town. The recent wave of remote work, then, has introduced a minefield of potential conflict.

Or has it? Folks, here's the surprise: Cramton's study was published in 2001.

The themes of human behavior remain the same, even as the tools and details change. The point here is that when people can row in the same boat, it solves a lot of collaboration challenges: It lets us communicate effortlessly. We all see each other's efforts. We share an obvious destination and can easily perceive progress. By contrast, when we can't be in the same room/boat together, the consequence is delays and misalignments and conflict.

The Zoom era largely precludes the same-room style of work.* But you can still honor the rowing-in-sync principle by encouraging "bursty communication," meaning that there are certain hours in the day that your team is standing by for real-time collaboration. (Even teams separated by many time zones can usually find an hour or two of overlap.)

Two researchers who studied remote teams found that "teams who communicate in bursts—exchanging messages quickly during

---

*Though, honestly, is it so crazy to invest in bringing dispersed team members together for a week or two to inaugurate some new change effort? My guess is that the benefits of the burst would far, far outweigh the travel costs.

periods of high activity—perform much better than remote teams whose conversations involve long lag time between responses and are spread across multiple topic threads."

That reference to "lag time" is critical. The researchers found that it's not distance that limits remote teams. It's delays. It's asynchronous communication that could have been synchronous.

Note that this doesn't mean your team needs to always be "on" and available. That can have its own negative consequences, since some work requires deep individual focus. Some bursts are long and continuous—design sprints require devoted energy for five consecutive days, and so did the radiology clinic story. But there are also more punctuated forms of bursts, as with the "bursty communication" principle. (And recall that the hospital receiving area story that began the book involved the team collaborating closely for one hour per day over 12 days.)

3.

To see how these ideas can fit together, consider how Matthew Knies handled the first few months of his tenure as leader of the Technical Data Center (TDC) team at ExxonMobil. When he joined the team in 2012, his first impressions were not promising. "It was a big room, and it was just full of shelf after shelf after shelf. And each one of those shelves was stacked with boxes and boxes of data." Everything from CDs to tape drives to USBs. Knies estimated there were probably petabytes (a petabyte is 1,000 terabytes) of data in the room—primarily seismic data from past subsurface explorations around the world.

The TDC team was the last stop for that data, responsible for receiving and preparing the files for long-term storage offsite. The data in the room was worth millions and millions of dollars. And

when Knies joined the team, it was in a state of utter disarray, he
said.

There was a *multiyear backlog* of files—meaning that it was going
to take them at least several years to clear the files that were on those
shelves. And while the files were in this "limbo" state—waiting for
their final home in the permanent archives—they could be hard
to locate. Someone would come in and say, "Hey, I'm looking for
Angola dataset block 17—do you have that dataset?" said Knies.
The team would poke around earnestly for the requested records,
but often the searches were fruitless. There were too many shelves
and too many boxes.

The consequences of this failure could be very expensive. Un-
able to locate the data, the company might have to go back to the
original vendor—the people who collected the original seismic
data, years earlier—and plead with them to provide a copy. (*Can you
send us a copy of that Angola data you created for us eight years ago?*) In
more than one case, the needless delay for data meant the company
risked missing out on a chance to make an educated bid on a particular business opportunity.

Knies remembers his boss being openly skeptical about the
group: *They just can't do anything.* The boss would actually walk
around the entire TDC area to get to the bathroom, even though
the most direct route was straight through it. He just couldn't
face it.

Knies, with the optimism that comes from being a first-time
manager, thought he could fix things. He set an ambitious goal: to
vanquish the backlog in 18 months. When he shared that aspiration
with the TDC team, they seemed polite but skeptical. Knies's boss
was less restrained: He laughed in Knies's face.

So pause there for a second: You're in charge of a team that's
stuck. What's your first move? You look for a Leverage Point. To

Knies, the obvious place to start was with archiving—the processing step that happened before the files were shipped offsite. The archiving process would allow them to clear out the boxes and files clogging up the shelves. That, in turn, would give the team a tangible payoff—kind of a seismic version of spring cleaning.

With that Leverage Point in mind, he *started with a burst*. He announced that every Thursday morning, the whole team would gather around the main table in the TDC area, and they'd all archive together. All day. "And they said, 'Yeah, but Laura works on her stuff and Dorothy works on her stuff. We all have different areas.' I said, 'Yeah, I know, but we're all going to do it together,'" Knies said.

Everybody at the same table, at the same time, with a common task—that's the spirit of a burst. The first Thursday, he brought in breakfast and sat down at the communal table with them. They were surprised to see him there—they weren't used to the boss archiving.

The truth was that he hadn't learned how to archive yet. So that day he made it his job to pull stickers off old tapes. Scrape off old barcodes so they could slap new ones on. Scrape, scrape, scrape, all day long. He joked that by the end of that Thursday, his fingertips had no skin on them.

The result? The team took two giant carts down to send off to long-term storage. "I will never forget the joy when I walked down to our shipping area with two of the guys," said Knies. "And they were just beaming. They were like, 'We have never archived this much, ever.'"

Every Thursday, they continued the work, and it was addictive, because the progress was so tangible. Two or three cartloads, every week. "Within just a matter of a couple of months, you can start to see holes through the shelves," said Knies. (Remember the progress principle from the introduction: "Of all the things that can boost emotions, motivation, and perceptions during a workday, the single most important is making progress in meaningful work.")

All of a sudden, it was possible to imagine a future with no backlog. A clear-shelf future.

4.

What Knies was doing—without realizing it—was honoring a motivational strategy that comes from Miguel Brendl, a professor of marketing at the University of Basel. "Early in your pursuit of your goal, look backwards at what you have achieved; toward the end, look forward," he told a reporter.

Brendl's idea makes intuitive sense: If you have a goal to lose 10 pounds, it's motivating to see those first few pounds drop off. *I lost one pound! Two!* Then, as you reach the halfway point, it seems more motivating somehow to flip your lens and start counting down to the goal: *Only four pounds left to go . . . three . . . two . . . one.*

So, in the case of Knies's team, the first revelation is that something (anything) is happening. Two carts get shipped out on the first day of work! That's like seeing those first two pounds drop off. *It's working!*

Then, as the team built up momentum, it generated more energy to look ahead to the end. *Imagine when we completely erase the whole backlog and the shelves are mostly bare.*

The ultimate effect of this "look backward, then look forward" strategy is to minimize the middle. Because in change efforts, the middle is the biggest trouble spot. In the beginning, there's an initial burst of energy: hope, novelty, adventure. It's the first few miles of a marathon. Then, later, you get a second burst as the finish line approaches: pride, satisfaction, relief.

But in the middle there's . . . nothing. Just a slow dog paddle forward, unbuoyed by the natural excitement of starts and finishes. It's the Battle of Midway.

As the motivation researcher Ayelet Fishbach puts it: "The only time we don't throw a party is in the middle." How do you counteract this motivational droop? Fishbach recommends that you *shorten the middle*.* Rather than think in terms of annual goals, where the "middle" might sprawl from February to November, you could think in terms of monthly or weekly goals. As each period resets, you get a burst of energy from the new beginning.

The discipline of agile—pervasive in software development—honors this principle. A development team might conduct sprints of two or three weeks—just enough time to crank out some meaningful improvements, but not so long that the middle starts to droop. It's like a methodology built around perpetual bursting. (There's more to come on agile in chapter 11.)

To get back to Knies and the Technical Data Center, the weekly archiving bursts were transforming the space. "The boss came by one day and said, 'Where did all the data go?'" said Knies. "He was floored."

Keeping the momentum going, Knies had the team switch to "file closing," a key bureaucratic process—but one that didn't have the same emotional payoff as seeing carts full of files disappear from the TDC. So he found ways to make the team's progress visible. At one point, he printed out a fundraising-style thermometer, coloring in the red line as they made progress toward the top. They kept working as a team, every Thursday.

Setting team-level goals, rather than individual ones, united

---

*Funny, my body-turnaround consultant keeps saying something similar to this . . .

their efforts. In the past, one woman (we'll call her Jane) had been notorious for telling other people: "Don't touch my files." Knies said that she was one of the best archivers in the group, but she had always stuck to her silo. He said the Thursday bursts transformed the way she worked. "All of a sudden, Jane was no longer interested in just Jane's files. Jane was interested in *everyone's* files," said Knies.

Knies's goal to finish the archiving in 18 months had seemed absurd. But they finished with months to spare. The biggest transformation, though, was within the team itself. "The TDC is no longer this team that nobody believes in," said Knies. "They became a team that believed in themselves. They became a team where they were proud of each other."

Together, they had sparked a reset that started around a table, one Thursday, with a concerted burst of work.

Whirlwind review: Chapter 6, Start with a Burst

1. The first way to Restack Resources on Leverage Points is to start with an intense burst of effort. Think of dislodging a stuck window.

2. Bursts are an antidote to the harms of "task switching"—continually moving back and forth between activities, which is inefficient and stressful.
    a. Brigid Schulte said her life felt like "time confetti."
    b. Confetti begets confetti: Ashley Whillans said, "When we feel time poor, we take on small, easy-to-complete tasks because they help us feel more control over our time."

3. The strategic use of protected blocks of time can spark quick change.
    a. In design sprints, the team members block their schedule for five days of collaboration.
    b. Even remote teams can embrace this by using "bursty communication"—reserving hours for real-time communication. Delays from asynchronous communication are the enemy.

4. A burst involves working to completion. Your team accomplishes something tangible—even if it's not "efficient."
    a. Greg McLawsen, helping his wife install a new hose system for the family garden, realized he needed to make another trip to Home Depot for a $2 part. It wasn't efficient but it was effective. It made his customer (aka wife) happy.

5. Bursts elevate the team's goals over the individual's. That can spark more team spirit and better collaboration.
    a. In ExxonMobil's Technical Data Center, the team managed to overcome a multiyear backlog of archives by starting a tradition of all-hands archiving, together, every Thursday.

6. The enemy of change efforts is the middle, when motivation lags. Bursts can help that by "shrinking the middle."
    a. Ayelet Fishbach: "The only time we don't throw a party is in the middle."

Recommendations (find live links at <u>danheath.com/reset-links</u>):

For more on "time confetti" (and how to avoid it), check out Brigid Schulte's book <u>Overwhelmed</u>, as well as Ashley Whillans's book <u>Time Smart</u>. You can read an excerpt here: <u>"Time Confetti and the Broken Promise of Leisure."</u> If you think a design sprint might help your team vault forward quickly, <u>Sprint</u> is a terrific resource. In this book, the authors detail the sprint method they developed at Google and which they've applied in organizations big and small around the world. For remote teams looking to accelerate their collaboration, here's an article on <u>the ways "bursty" communication can help your team thrive</u>. If the "middle problem" of motivation resonated with you, it's worth picking up a copy of <u>Get It Done</u> by Ayelet Fishbach. She draws on the burgeoning field of motivation science to develop a framework for navigating personal change. Another strategy for combatting the murky middle is to "multiply milestones," which means finding intermediate achievements worthy of celebrating. My brother and I devote a chapter to that topic in our book <u>The Power of Moments</u>.

7

RECYCLE WASTE

>> You can Restack Resources on your Leverage Points by ending work that doesn't serve the mission.

RECYCLE WASTE

1.

The leaders in the City of Asheboro in North Carolina wanted to reduce their fuel costs. One area that consumed a lot of fuel was trash collection. They couldn't stop or delay trash collection—that's the kind of move that reliably riles up citizens. But by analyzing the system as a whole, they hoped they'd spot inefficiencies. (*Map the system.*)

They had a fleet of regular trash trucks that drove block by block to pick up trash. In addition, they had two bulk trash trucks capable of picking up larger items such as mattresses or fridges. Plus an additional two brush/yard waste trucks that would retrieve big tree limbs, bagged piles of leaves, and so on. Just like the normal trash trucks, these four "special" trucks would drive up and down every street in the city.

What the Asheboro leaders realized, in their investigation, was that the special trucks didn't have many customers. How often do you throw out an old fridge? So the bulk trucks were driving routes where the vast majority of miles (and thus gallons of fuel) were wasted.

Inspired, the city's IT team commissioned a mobile device that could be used by the regular sanitation workers. When they encountered a house that needed a special pickup—a mattress or a tree limb—the crew would just press a button on the device, which would log the GIS coordinates for that house. They were laying a digital breadcrumb trail for the bulk-trash team.

Suddenly, those four special trucks didn't have to drive down every single block. They could just drive point to point, since all the addresses had been logged by their colleagues. As a result, the City of Asheboro saved thousands of dollars in gas and reduced wear and tear on their trucks. They cut waste.

"Waste" is a word with a lot of associations: Garbage. Landfills. "A waste of time." But in this book, I want to use a version of the term prevalent in the world of lean thinking (and mentioned briefly in the introduction), which says: Waste is anything that doesn't add value to your work in the customer's eyes.

Let's say Asheboro saved a thousand gallons of gas with its innovative point-to-point system. That counts as trimming waste because the citizens served didn't care what routes these trucks drove en route to picking up their bulk trash. By contrast, if Asheboro had saved a thousand gallons of gas by limiting or delaying the bulk pickups, that would *not* be trimming waste, because people find it valuable to have their dirty old futons picked up as quickly as possible.

Many organizations use the acronym DOWNTIME—inspired by the Toyota Production System, which for operations researchers is sort of like the Holy of Holies—to capture eight possible categories of waste:

Defects

Overproduction

Waiting

Nonutilized talent

Transportation

Inventory

Motion

Excess processing

The Asheboro trash truck story, for example, showcases how you can reduce waste in the category of Transportation.

To illustrate all eight elements, let's analyze waste in a hypothetical bakery:

Defects: Burned cookies, sad shriveled croissants

Overproduction: The donuts thrown out at the end of the day

Waiting: The worker twiddling thumbs, waiting for dough to rise

Nonutilized talent: A cake decorator washing dishes

Transportation: The flour bag being stored too far from the mixer, requiring it to be moved back and forth constantly

Inventory: Overbought milk that went bad

Motion (the people version of Transportation): The counter staff's thousands of unnecessary steps going back and forth from the register to the distant coffeepot

Excess processing: Birthday cakes being iced using an obscure French technique that pleases the pastry chef but goes unnoticed by the customer, who just wants their kid's name spelled right

This DOWNTIME model is grounded in the factory world, so it may not translate completely to your world. (Still, I find it pretty easy to find examples of writing "waste" that fit most of the categories above.)* The particulars of the model are not as important as its central message: Wasteful activities can come in many colors.

Restacking Resources on your Leverage Points can be painful, because most of the resource shifting we do will involve making trade-offs. (Remember: "Change is not AND, it's INSTEAD OF.") Even if we know we're making a wise trade-off, it can still come with a sting. Extra time spent on your marriage is time not spent jockeying for a promotion. Extra money spent on car repair is not available for family vacations.

But there's no sting when it comes to waste. The old cliché goes, "There's no free lunch," but that's not quite true. *Waste is a free lunch.*† If we can spot waste, we can immediately recycle those resources—money, energy, labor, materials—to push harder on our Leverage Points. And there's no downside! Because the customer (by definition) did not value the things that you cut back.

That's why waste is worth obsessing about.

2.

At Sweetgreen, the salad restaurant, staff had always mixed customers' orders in big metal bowls. The bowls cost a lot and they had to be washed between uses, which consumed a lot of water and energy and dishwashing labor. So somebody wondered, *Hey, what if we didn't need these bowls?*

Your first thought might be: *Let the customer mix their own salad.*

---

*Maybe a more accurate writer's acronym would be DUMPS, involving Distraction, Undermotivation, Missed deadlines, Procrastination, and Self-hatred

†Eww but true.

Ah, but wait: Mixing the salad *does* add value, at least for many customers, so it's not a wasteful activity.

Customers don't really care *where* their salad is mixed, though. What if you could just mix their salad in the takeout bowls? No transfers required, no washing.

Sweetgreen tested that idea, but the staffers found that the typical takeout bowls were too shallow and small to allow for easy mixing. (DOWNTIME: Defects in spilled salad; Excess processing in slower times.) So instead, the chain commissioned a larger hexagonal to-go bowl that was conducive to mixing.

The metal bowls were shelved. Poof, waste eliminated. But notice that eliminating waste required seeing the whole system. (*Map the system.*) To the people mixing the salads, the metal bowls seemed necessary. To the dishwashers, they seemed inevitable. Habits conceal waste.

I started thinking about my parenting through the lens of waste. One day I was replaying in my head the morning routine of getting my two young daughters ready for school. There was plenty of waste. Nagging is waste. Fussing is waste. Crying is waste. And that was just me—my daughters were doing plenty of wasteful things, too.

I imagined what a map of our movements would look like, in the spirit of those spaghetti charts from chapter 5: Countless trips up and down the stairs to retrieve shoes or socks. (DOWNTIME: Motion.) Sometimes, my daughters would filibuster my wife and me long enough that, feeling rushed, we'd end up tying their shoes for them, even though they're fully capable. (DOWNTIME: Nonutilized talent.)

So my wife schemed up one systemic improvement: She piled all the girls' shoes and socks—including a frankly disturbing quantity of Crocs—into a big drawer by the back door. Now there are no more socks or shoes upstairs. As a bonus, we don't get dirt tracked through the house because now they take off their shoes when they come inside and dump them in the drawer. That saves needless cleaning. (DOWNTIME: Excess processing.)

As a result of our antiwaste efforts, our morning habits have improved meaningfully, which has freed up extra time to argue about whether it's safe to eat the brown spot on the waffle. (DOWN-TIME: Defects.)

3.

Waste is a familiar concept in the business canon. Anyone who's ever sat through a lean, six sigma, or kaizen training will know the idea well. If you want the deep dive on the subject, good news, there is an entire internet full of waste-related content waiting for you, along with countless consultants standing by, ready to help.

Our purpose here, though, is not necessarily to make your enterprise more efficient in the long term, which is often the goal of waste reduction. Our purpose is to help you reset—get you unstuck and moving. You're hoping to put some points on the board in weeks or months, not quarters or years.

In keeping with that, you've got to stay focused on waste that can be quickly harvested and repurposed. You're looking for hours, dollars, and resources that can be redeployed immediately from one purpose to another.

Remember the hospital receiving area from the introduction, and the frequent calls to the red phone? ("Where's my package??") Every time Suett and his team *stopped* one of those calls from happening, they recycled waste. They took five minutes from a non-value-added activity and made it available for value-added activity—which, notice, made it more likely that they'd prevent even more of those package-seeking calls in the future. They banked some quick wins.

The pastor Graham Standish was looking for quick wins in his worship service. In an era of declining church attendance, it's a struggle to keep a congregation engaged and loyal. Standish had some compelling ideas about how to freshen up the service, but often the changes would meet resistance from longtime members. Swapping out classic hymns for contemporary ones, for example, drew complaints from some old-timers.

But he identified something that he was sure no one would miss: the dead time during the worship service. First, he cut out "watching": He explained, "It's typical in a church that when someone finishes a prayer or something, we watch them walk back to their seat. And once they sit down, the next person stands and walks to the front. [But now we have] trained people to be right at the front and ready to go. So no 'watching.'"

That shaved a few idle minutes from the service. He also changed the way announcements were handled. In the past, a bunch of announcements were read aloud, then Standish would ask whether anyone had additional announcements. Long delay. Sometimes, someone in the back would raise their hand and say something that no one could hear. Standish would repeat it. In the new model, Standish would only make the most critical announcements, and he trained the congregation to rely on the bulletin for smaller issues.

Standish even flagged the kind of ceremonial preambles that people would often use at the podium: "As we begin our service this morning, let us come to God with a sense of prayerful readiness . . ." he joked.

The effect of these tweaks? He managed to trim 5 to 10 minutes from the service time without cutting any of the actual *worship*. "People commented to me how they didn't know what was different, but it just felt like the service was more seamless," he said. "One person said to me, 'I just love how everything just seems to fit together and how well everyone works together.'"

The service felt zippier, and the church members were able to leave earlier, which gave them a precious head start in beating other congregations to local restaurants for Sunday lunch.

4.

In nonfactory environments, probably the most critical component of the DOWNTIME framework is the N: Nonutilized talent.* This category includes idle time. Distracted time. But its most profound meaning is this: *It's wasteful when people are playing below their level.*

As an example, recall the Gartner story from chapter 3 on *studying bright spots*. Ken Davis discovered that the critical Leverage Point, in keeping clients happy and likely to renew was getting them on the phone with client partners. The best use of a client partner's time, then, was a call with a client.

Given that realization, it became clear that *scheduling* calls was a wasteful activity for the client partners. That's Nonutilized talent. Because a lot of people were capable of scheduling calls—or the scheduling could be automated.

What the client partners were uniquely good at was helping clients, live, with their business challenges. A minute stolen from "scheduling calls" and added to "helping clients" was a win. That's the spirit of *recycling waste*.

---

*I had to chuckle about the clunky phrase "Nonutilized talent." "Underutilized talent" would probably be a little less neuron-grating, but unfortunately then you'd be stuck with DOWUTIME as your mnemonic. I can appreciate a good acronym-shoehorning when I see it, as a serial offender myself . . .

When you clear lower-value activities from people's schedules to free them up for higher-value ones, let's call that "shifting right." That's a term I learned from Gary Kaplan, the president of AXA XL's construction-insurance business.

To understand how Kaplan has implemented "shift right," it helps to know a bit about his business. For construction companies, who are Kaplan's customers, there is a long list of risks for which they might want to buy insurance. Such as: Workers getting hurt. Accidental polluting of the area. Subcontractors defaulting and leaving the project in the lurch. And more.

Kaplan's group wants to sell insurance for these risks, but that requires a lot of judgment, since there aren't millions of data points to rely on, as there might be for life insurance. Underwriters are the people who wield that judgment. They determine how much to charge potential clients for their unique risks. To provide liability insurance for worker's accidents, for instance, the underwriters would ask a lot of questions about workplace safety practices. If they learned that the construction foreman was obsessive about safety, then they'd charge less for insurance coverage.

So Kaplan started working with underwriters to understand their work. He teased apart the underwriters' objective work—fact-based, black-and-white—from their subjective work, which required judgment. The objective work could be shifted right, transferred to support staffers or outsourced, but the subjective work couldn't.

"You want the underwriter to use their brain and their understanding of the customer to help you decide what range of that pricing they should select: the high end or the low end," said Kaplan. That's the subjective work that only the underwriters can do.

As a result of this ongoing shift-right work, the average underwriter in Kaplan's group went from managing $4 million in policy premiums to managing $14 million. That's a *tripling* in productivity that emerged from elevating people to the top of their range.

How could you help your team "shift right"? With the rise of ChatGPT and Claude and other AI models, organizations have begun searching for ways to augment the productivity of their workers.* As one example among many, AI tools can help recruiters do the initial scanning on a flood of incoming résumés for an open position. Or AI chatbots can field the simplest inquiries for a customer support center.

A word of caution, though: While this shift-right mentality can be both productive and elevating—helping everyone play at the top of their game—it can certainly be taken too far.

Some version of this philosophy has led to the factory mindset of modern health care, in which doctors seem to have less and less time with every patient they see. Only doctors can diagnose patients, the thinking goes, so let's shift right everything else: greeting the patient and weighing them and taking their case history and checking their blood pressure and so on.

This is compelling logic—up to a point. It really does seem wasteful for the doctor to weigh a patient. But human beings are not factories with legs. I love writing but I would not like to have my schedule purged of research and thinking and teaching so that I could become a pure, optimized prose monkey, maximizing the output of words per hour.

If this seems like a morally fraught issue, it need not be. It's really not hard to separate enlightened shifting-right from contemptible

---

*I was hopeful that I could get ChatGPT to shoulder the burden of writing this book, allowing me to "shift right" to napping and Wordle. Never could quite figure out how to use its talents, though. Maybe next book.

shifting-right. Just ask the people affected! (At Gartner, client partners were *happy* not to have to schedule calls.)

People will tell you what's good for them, if you care enough
to ask.

5.

In Ed Catmull's fascinating book, *Creativity, Inc.*—Catmull is the
co-founder of Pixar—he tells the story of arriving at Disney Anima-
tion and discovering that the creative team was basically at war with
the "oversight group," which was chartered with ensuring that the
creatives stayed on time and on budget. The creative team bristled
under this supervision. "They felt they no longer had the flexibil-
ity they needed to respond quickly to problems because the oversight group nitpicked every decision—even the tiniest decision—to
death," said Catmull. "They felt powerless."

So Catmull and the producer John Walker made a surprising
decision: They eliminated the oversight group.

But was that wise? Wouldn't it introduce a lot of risk into the
production? Here is how Catmull analyzed the decision:

> We believed that the production people were conscientious
> managers who were trying to bring a complex project in on
> time and on budget. In our view, the oversight group added
> nothing to the process but tension. The micromanagement
> they imposed was of no value, since the production people al-
> ready had a set of limits that determined their every move—
> the overall budget and the deadline. Within that, they needed
> all the flexibility they could get.

The level of oversight, in his telling, was wasteful. To return to the DOWNTIME framework: Micromanagement is a toxic combination of *Excess processing* (too much management per unit of work) and *Nonutilized talent* (restricting the creatives' ability to use their full range of talents).

Another example of excessive oversight came from an account executive at a SaaS software company, who told me about the insane amount of time his team spends *forecasting* sales: "We're supposed to sit there, for probably 30 minutes every day, just entering data. Then we have a weekly hour-long call to review that data. Then our leaders spend at least 90 minutes a week on another call, reviewing that data with our VPs. Our VPs then go review that data with our EVPs and CRO . . . every single week. All these calls are staggered throughout the week, so leaders will ping their subordinates for clarifying details every day, who will then ping their subordinates to further clarify, then that update gets rolled back up to the VP, etc. etc. . . . One VP told me he's on 18 hours of forecasting calls every week. Every. Single. Week."

The point of this is not that oversight is bad. (I wrote a book called *Upstream* that heroicizes people who try to stop problems before they happen, so believe me, I get the value of oversight and compliance!) Rather, as the old saying goes, *The dose makes the poison*. Eighteen hours of forecasting calls every week is not a wise dose of oversight. It's a continual toilet-flushing of human potential.

So how can we learn to distinguish "wise oversight" from "wasteful oversight"? A useful clarification comes from Jeff Bezos. In a shareholder letter, he compared "Type 1" and "Type 2" decisions.

Type 1 decisions, in his terminology, "are consequential and irreversible or nearly irreversible—one-way doors—and these decisions must be made methodically, carefully, slowly, with great deliberation and consultation. If you walk through and don't like what you see on the other side, you can't get back to where you were before."

Type 2 decisions, though, are reversible. Two-way streets. If you make a decision and you don't like the results, you just undo it. "Type 2 decisions can and should be made quickly by high judgment individuals or small groups," wrote Bezos.

Bezos warned that in many organizations, the two types of decisions get confused or conflated. "As organizations get larger, there seems to be a tendency to use the heavy-weight Type 1 decision-making *process* on most decisions, including many Type 2 decisions," he wrote. "The end result of this is slowness, unthoughtful risk aversion, failure to experiment sufficiently, and consequently diminished invention."

Some decisions, Bezos is saying, really do deserve the slow, cautious approach. Mergers, acquisitions, major pricing shifts, potential layoffs, and more. Take your time, get it right. But most decisions—such as how to animate a scene in a cartoon, or how to forecast this week's sales activity—are easily reversible and shouldn't be bogged down by excessive process. Using a Type 1 process on Type 2 decisions is simply wasteful.

In this chapter, we've seen myriad ways that waste can be recaptured: Recaptured fuel from smarter trash-truck routes. Recaptured minutes from sluggish church services. Recaptured time for underwriters. And recaptured energy and motivation for henpecked animators. The quest to recapture waste is a theme that will continue to thread through the material that follows.

Next up: What happens when you've repurposed all the waste and you still need more fuel? Inevitably, in the absence of new resources, you'll have to cut back on something. How do you make those trade-offs in the least painful way possible?

Whirlwind review: Chapter 7, Recycle Waste

1. The second way to Restack Resources is to capture "waste," which is any activity that doesn't add value in the customer's eyes.

   a. *In Asheboro, waste was cut by using technology that allowed bulk trash trucks to follow point-to-point routes for customer pickups.*

2. Waste comes in many varieties, and it's worth obsessing about, because waste offers a free lunch: You can Restack Resources with no painful trade-off.

   a. *The DOWNTIME framework expands our thinking about the many kinds of waste: Defects, Overproduction, Waiting, Nonutilized talent, Transportation, Inventory, Motion, and Excess processing.*

   b. *As an example, Sweetgreen cut waste by mixing salads directly in the customers' bowls.*

3. In nonfactory environments, a critical area of waste is people playing below their level. You can correct that by "shifting right."

   a. *At AXA XL, Gary Kaplan consciously cleared his people's plates of lower-value activities so they could focus on what they did best.*

4. One note of caution: Shifting right can be taken too far. It can lead to soul-deadening overspecialization, as with the factory mindset of modern health care. But you can get it right on your team: People will tell you what's good for them, if you ask them.

5. Micromanagement is another near-universal kind of waste.

   a. *Ed Catmull eliminated the "oversight group" that was nitpicking the creatives.*

   b. *A sales VP at one company logged 18 hours of forecasting calls every week.*

6. How do you distinguish proper oversight from *wasteful* oversight? Jeff Bezos distinguished Type 1 decisions (big and nearly irreversible) from Type 2 decisions (readily reversible). It's best not to overthink Type 2 situations.

Recommendations (find live links at danheath.com/reset-links):

Want a reminder of the DOWNTIME categories? Here is one two-page printable handout from the Eureka Institute that I especially liked. Also, remember the story of the hospital receiving area? Part of their miraculous transformation was DOWNTIME-driven. Here's the business school case study. (The teaching note, for educators only, has the full DOWNTIME analysis.) For a less practical and more theoretical foray into lean manufacturing more generally, you might take a look at _The Machine That Changed the World_. It'll give you an overview of the evolution of lean, plus a deeper sense of why lean operations succeed where others fail. As an aside, Gary Kaplan (the AXA XL/"shift right" guy) is a champion of a methodology called "Rapid Results," which he discusses briefly here. In short, Rapid Results sets up ambitious 100-day challenges that are led by self-managing teams. Though not waste-specific, the Rapid Results approach is certainly relevant to our overall mission to get rolling, and though I don't write about it, it was one of the methodologies that informed the book's framework. Finally, you can enjoy the full, director's-cut version of Catmull's mission to protect Pixar's creatives in his book, _Creativity, Inc_. It's a great book and has lots of behind-the-scenes tales about movies such as _Toy Story, Finding Nemo,_ and _WALL-E._

DO LESS <u>AND</u> MORE

>> You can Restack Resources on
your Leverage Points by shifting effort from
lower-value work to higher-value.

DO LESS <u>AND</u> MORE

1.

Rosa's daughter Mia had recently been diagnosed with attention deficit hyperactivity disorder (ADHD). Mia was doing better in school—the return to in-person school, postpandemic, had helped her—and Rosa wanted to keep the momentum going at home. But Rosa was starting to feel overwhelmed, especially in the mornings. She and her husband, Sal, had to get ready for work and get Mia, plus her two sisters, off for school and day care. Rosa and Sal found themselves constantly yelling and barking orders at their children to finish breakfast and get ready to leave. It was the worst possible way to start the day—chaotic and tense—especially for Mia, who would react to the stress by acting out even more.

Rosa had read up on how parents could help children with ADHD, but she found herself reacting in the moment, losing patience. It challenged Rosa's confidence as a parent—she didn't want to be part of the problem. Sal and Rosa had briefly considered medication for Mia but they were extremely wary of it—Mia was only seven years old.

Rosa made an appointment with John J. Murphy, a solutions-focused therapist. Early in their first session, Murphy asked her about the bright spots in their relationship—the times when Mia behaved well. Here's how the conversation went from there, as recounted in Murphy's book *Solution-Focused Therapy*:

ROSA: There are times when Mia listens and minds better, and it's easier interacting with her. She's very task oriented when you give her jobs. She loves to help. She craves attention, so when you do give her positive attention, she responds well. If I've got a craft activity planned or I'm baking something she can help with, or playing a game with her, she can be a model child. When we do things like that, it's definitely better. But it's just not always possible to give her the level of attention she craves. That's when she'll find other ways to get attention, and that's when the trouble starts.

THERAPIST: It's interesting how she responds so well to the positive attention you give her. Like a model child, as you said. That's a high compliment coming from a parent.

ROSA: (smiles) Yeah, she's good during those times. She's definitely capable of it.

THERAPIST: It sounds like you're both capable of making that happen.

ROSA: It's just getting her to be more like that when she's not getting the attention.

THERAPIST: Yes. So, these events and times are happening, just maybe not as often, or, uh, in as many situations, as you would like?

ROSA: Yes.

THERAPIST: I'm curious what else you do, or other people do, or anything else that helps make these events and times happen more.

ROSA: Hmm. Let's see. . . . Getting to bed at a decent time definitely helps me wake up quicker and feel better, you know, more energy, less irritable. I'm more patient with Mia and everybody else. The same for Sal. Sometimes we both stay up too late, and we end up regretting it in the morning.

As the conversation continued, Rosa and Murphy identified a number of possible Leverage Points to make things better, including "setting out her children's clothes the night before school, going to bed a little earlier, setting her alarm to wake up 20 or 30 minutes before waking the kids, and occasionally initiating a game or craft with Mia in the evening."

When Rosa came back for her next session, she reported a dramatic improvement. She had tried a bunch of different things and the one that worked best, she reported, was waking up before the kids. "Just being able to sit and breathe a little in the morning, have a cup of coffee in peace before the chaos starts. It puts me in a more positive mindset. . . . I can be more chill with Mia, my kids, my husband."

She actually discontinued therapy soon thereafter: Her relationship with Mia wasn't perfect, but it was a lot better.

Rosa improved a critical relationship after one therapy session! That's getting unstuck quickly (although perhaps not a great business model for therapists). How did it happen? First, Rosa and Murphy identified some possible Leverage Points by *studying bright spots*. Notice how the therapist draws her attention to the times Rosa is *already* succeeding: "sounds like you're both capable of making that happen."

Then, Rosa immediately Restacked her Resources to support them. In this case, that meant changing the way she spent her time: choosing to wake up 20–30 minutes before her kids, which in turn meant going to bed earlier.

Notice this was not a costless decision. To accommodate that extra time in the morning—to summon her Zen place before the chaos began—she had to skimp on time with Sal the night before. There was no "waste" to recycle here. The time swap was a trade-off, and it stung.

This chapter is devoted to that core trade-off: less of this, more of that. And what we're chasing, in particular, is a way to *minimize the sting* of those trade-offs. In Rosa's situation, she faced what was effectively a zero-sum trade: time in the evening for time in the morning.

But in organizations it's not always zero-sum like that. If you know where to look, you can find low-sting, high-bang trade-offs.

2.

David Philippi's firm, Strategex, grounds its work in the Pareto principle, the idea that 80% of the outputs/consequences come from 20% of the inputs/causes. Philippi's job is to help clients distinguish the 20% from the 80%, and then to change their operations based on those insights.

In one case, Philippi and his team were working with a manufacturer of optical instruments. The company had about 3,500 customers, mostly military, aerospace, and health care organizations. Some number crunching revealed that 10% of those customers yielded 80% of the revenue.

When it came to profit, though, the numbers were even more stark. The company's top set of customers were generating *more* *than all* of the company's profit.* In other words, the great majority of the company's customers were unprofitable.

"The fallacy that most people believe is that 20% of customers or products are 80% of the profits," said Philippi. "And that's not true. What we find is that those 20% of customers—that are 80% of the revenue—are generally 150% of the profit. So what we tell our clients from the get-go is: Your problem isn't that you're not making enough. It's that you're not keeping it."

Philippi has found that his clients make twin mistakes: They undercoddle their best customers and overcoddle their worst. Often those mistakes derive from a noble desire: These companies aspire to treat customers the same. And treating people equally is a great goal for, say, craps dealers. Or democracy. But to treat a $1 million customer the same as a $100 customer? It's like treating your hamster the same as your daughter because they're both mammals.

Philippi finds that, paradoxically, the biggest customers are often treated *worse* than the smallest. "One of the questions we ask clients is: What's your on-time delivery rate for those critical few customers—the 20% that are 80% of the revenue?" he said. "And it was shocking to me, but what we generally find is that the on-time

---

*What does it mean for some customers to generate "more than all" of a company's profit? Consider a tax prep firm with three customers who pay $100 each. Customers A and B have straightforward situations. It costs about $60 apiece to serve them, so they each generate $40 in profit. Meanwhile, Customer C's situation is complex—and he is also hard to communicate with—meaning a lot of time is burned. It costs $120 to serve him, for a loss of $20. So the firm as a whole has revenue of $300 (100 + 100 + 100) and profit of $60 (40 + 40 − 20). So note that Customers A and B, together, make up *more than all* of the company's profit, because if the business had not served Customer C, then the total profit would have been $80 instead of $60.

delivery rates are far better with the smaller customers than they are with their largest customers."

The reason? Their orders are simpler. It's easier to get 1 piece shipped out than a complicated assembly involving 100 pieces. But if the shipping team is measured on the *percentage of on-time deliveries*, then that provides a perverse incentive to neglect the hard cases. They can ace the 97 easy deliveries, deprioritize the 3 hard ones, and look like geniuses (97% on-time rate!).

Once you catch on to this pattern, you can easily fix it. You make sure that all shipments are *not* treated equally. For your top customers, the on-time rate should be perfect: 100%. Always and forever. That's how you keep them loyal and encourage them to do more business with you.

Meanwhile, what should you do about the mass of overcoddled customers? Philippi says that clients are often fearful about changing those relationships. *Aren't we going to ruin our business if we tell some customers "no"?**

He reassures them that it's not about telling some customers to

---

*In writing this chapter, it occurred to me—to my chagrin—that I was an "overcoddled customer" at my local coffee shop. For years, the shop had sold a bottomless cup of coffee, with free self-service refills. This was perfect for me—and also for a tribe of older people who met every morning and drank about six cups apiece, then spent the rest of the morning in the bathroom. But as the coffee shop got more crowded, no doubt we looked less valuable as customers. The "bottomless cup" people like me were hogging tables that could have been used by the "sit down and have a quick breakfast" people. So the owners changed the policy. No more self-service, no more refills. You want another cup of coffee? Pay for it. I was totally incensed about this shift at the time. The injustice! But now I see clearly that it was the right move for the owners. And you know what? I still go there every day.

buzz off. The point is to ensure that customers are paying for the resources they're consuming. There are many ways to approach this: Raise prices. Create a minimum order size. Set lower expectations for things like delivery time. Offer self-service tools.

It's your job to define the "offer" for your customers. It's their job to accept or decline. If there are customers who huff and puff about your new offer and take their business elsewhere, take heart: You've won a double victory. You've taken some unprofitable customers off your ledger and added them to your competitor's.

This is Restacking Resources. To get unstuck and start moving again, you need to free up resources, and Strategex is showing you how: Steal from the overcoddled and give to the undercoddled.

Here's a haunting thought: What if the story is the same in our personal lives? What if we are undercoddling the most important people and overcoddling the least? Philippi brought up this issue with me: "If you look at why marriages struggle or why people struggle, they're generally spread too thin. Trying to do too much and not spending the amount of time they need to on those critical core issues. Sometimes it's money, but a lot of times it's, boy, we're doing too many things. . . . Whenever we try to do too much, it steals time away from the things that matter most."

Philippi and his team use a force-ranking process with business clients that we might adapt for our personal lives as well. They'll rank-order the client's customers from best to worst and then group them into quartiles. As we've seen, the bottom quartile of customers is almost always unprofitable. You would literally have a better business, in almost all respects (other than perhaps top-line revenue), by cutting them loose.

My guess is that if you did a similar force-ranking analysis of the relationships in your life, you'd find similar dynamics in the bottom quartile. You'd find relationships that cause a lot of stress, or that consume a lot of time, without a commensurate return of meaning or happiness.

Is this suggestion too mercenary? To be clear, you need not rank people according to "what you get from them," like a business might. ("I'm sorry, son, but you're insufficiently profitable to deserve your current allocation of affection.") Nor do you need to rank people according to who makes you happiest. If you regularly visit an older relative at a nursing home, for instance, you probably don't get many giggles from the experience, but it's not about that.

The point is: You're the one who gets to set the scoreboard!

For Philippi, it's his wife and kids who are at the top of the charts. He tries to make decisions accordingly. In the spring of 2024, he led a two-day training session near his home in the Chicago area. After the first day ended, the client invited him to dinner. Rather than make up an excuse, he tried leveling with them.

"I've got three kids," he explained. "My oldest son, he's 12—he wants to play Ping-Pong. My middle daughter wants to play Super Mario Brothers. My youngest—he's a soccer player, he wants me to play goalie. So thank you very much for the invitation, but I want to go home and spend time with them. Because there's gonna come a day that they're not gonna want to do these things anymore."

That night, after sessions of soccer and Super Mario Bros., the two younger kids got to bed. Now it was time for Ping-Pong. During the game, his son told him, "Dad, I tried out for the school play, and there's gonna be lots of auditions. So I don't think we can play Ping-Pong anymore."

And it struck Philippi: *I knew the day was coming but I didn't know it was going to be tonight!*

"I got the last match in with my son," he said. He was thankful not to have traded that for a client dinner.

"Every day we have a choice," said Philippi.

3.

As the Ping-Pong story makes clear, the Pareto-style analysis used by Strategex is not exclusive to revenue and profit. Your goals might have nothing to do with juicing business results. Maybe you're trying to keep employees more engaged or serve the homeless better or overhaul federal wetlands policy.

Whatever direction you're pushing, you need to Find a Leverage Point and Restack Resources on it. And Strategex is showing us that, with the right analysis, we can *reliably* find places where we're spending too many resources and other places where we're spending too few. That analysis can apply not just to profits but to donors or programs or employee benefits or campaign activities.

Strategex's approach can be data-intensive—trawling through thousands of customer records. But there are less rigorous ways to arrive at similar conclusions. My guess is that any nonprofit's staff could tell you confidently which donors are "overcoddled." Any school's staff could tell you which parents are overcoddled. No big-data analysis needed.

Here's a simple tool for separating areas that "need more" from areas that "need less." I learned it from a friend, who used this exercise at an offsite and reported that it sparked really useful discussion. Basically, you draw quadrants on a whiteboard with the following labels:

You can fill in the quadrants with any kind of "thing":

→ STOP: *The policy that it's okay to bring pets to work. It's getting smelly and weird.*

→ START: *Using an outside law firm to handle contracts. It's a constraint internally.*

→ MORE: *Inside sales efforts in the Southeast. It's working.*

→ LESS: *Ginning up employee social events. Not many people seem to care.*

My friend said the hardest quadrants to address were LESS and, especially, STOP. Which is predictable. Usually, when we think about making changes, we're thinking about adding something. New ideas, new initiatives, new investments. But we've got to remember the mantra: Change is not AND, it's INSTEAD OF. Less of this, more of that.

That "INSTEAD OF" mindset was the heart of the turnaround strategy used by Art Mollenhauer, after he accepted the role of CEO of the Big Brothers Big Sisters of Metropolitan Chicago

(BBBS-MC) in 2006. When he took over, the organization was in bleak shape. Basically insolvent.

It had been surviving week to week on board members' credit cards and life-support payments from the national organization. Mismanaged for years, the Chicago chapter was failing at its core mission, which was to invest in at-risk youth by matching them with mentors.

Mollenhauer knew what he was getting into. He had basically quadrupled the length of the job-interview process at his own request. He flew to the national office on his own dime. He sat in on a board meeting. He signed up to be a volunteer and made a $25 donation to experience the organization from the outside. (*Go and see the work.*) He even met with the organization's anxious bankers, who let him know that the organization had used 95% of its credit limit.

Early in his tenure, he met with major donors to convince them that better times were coming. He challenged board members to pony up to support the turnaround—offering to match their contributions one-to-one *with his own money*!

Meanwhile, he forced a reassessment of the organization's programs, which were both plentiful and ineffective. Mollenhauer asked: Which of our programs are delivering on our mission? And which are providing a financial contribution? Programs that did neither were discontinued, no matter how well-intentioned. About a fifth of BBBS-MC's programs were mothballed within months of Mollenhauer taking the job.

On another front, he assessed the organization's staff and board members. "It was pretty apparent that there were some great assets in the organization," he said. "There were also some people, on the other hand, that had to go. And had to go fairly quickly."

Within a month, a third of the board and a quarter of the staff

were gone. Some left voluntarily, and others were fired. Mollenhauer looked at every resulting vacancy as an opportunity—a
chance for renewal, a chance to replace an underperformer with a
star.

Much of Mollenhauer's early work, then, was devoted to stanch-
ing the organizational bleeding: Reducing expenses. Cutting the
programmatic deadwood. Firing underperformers. Reassuring nervous bankers.

But even as he worked on the "crisis" side of the ledger, he was
investing in new opportunities as well. (Not just STOP + LESS
but also START + MORE.) He arranged an expensive board retreat at Northwestern University, believing that the board needed
to start acting like the forward-looking entity it aspired to become.
He created a new role—a corporate partnership manager—and
hired someone, to the tune of $60,000. "Chicago has an amazing
corporate presence," said Mollenhauer. "I thought we had a great
opportunity to really grow."

One of his most striking moves concerned the organization's offices. For context, corporate real estate is often graded as Class A,
B, or C. Class C properties, in the description of one real estate
website, are "barely functional" and "cheap to rent"—in the "wan-
ing days of their useful life."

The organization's offices at that time were, Mollenhauer joked,
a Class C-minus.

"The elevators were constantly breaking down," he said. "The
sewage was constantly backing up. . . . And what was fascinating is a
lot of the corporate board members were kind of saying, 'Well, this
is how it is in a nonprofit. Gritty, you know, we don't spend a lot on
offices and overhead.' And I saw all these people, hardworking staff,
in a very deficient place."

Mollenhauer thought: *We've gotta get a new office.* Because the decrepitude of the place somehow symbolized the organization's state. *This is what we deserve. This is who we are.* It was almost like a heavy-handed metaphor: *We stink.*

But the timing for an upgrade was rough. Mollenhauer realized it took a certain amount of chutzpah to pitch the board a long-term contract for new office space, even as he was laying off staff and pledging financial responsibility to bankers. He persisted, though. *We can't get so consumed with short-term issues that we forget to think about the future,* he argued.

It helped his case when, on the day he pitched the new office idea, four board members got stuck in the elevator. And the air conditioner broke down. And sewage was clearly visible in the washrooms. Some board members wondered whether Mollenhauer had set it all up.

Ultimately, the board greenlit the request, and the search began for an office that better fit their aspirations. And that was free of open sewage.

With Mollenhauer pushing change on every front, the turnaround didn't take long: Within 40 days, they'd paid off their line of credit. ("I think the banker almost cried, we did it so quickly," quipped Mollenhauer.) Within about a year, to the delight of the employees, they moved into their new office. "People felt like they were valued and treasured," he said.

And the newly hired corporate partnership manager landed a deal with Bank of America, which included a $30,000 grant. "We celebrated the heck out of that with our board and our staff," said Mollenhauer. "We said, 'I know we've had trouble, but Bank of America is a very serious organization.'" It was a strong vote of confidence in the new direction.

4.

What I want to underscore about Mollenhauer's work is the idea that in the early stages of change, you've got to be ambidextrous: Both cutting and investing. Both defense and offense. LESS and MORE.

This is a theme echoed by other turnaround experts. "You cannot save your way to health," said Michael M. Kaiser in *The Art of the Turnaround,* his excellent book discussing how he turned around prestigious arts organizations, including the Royal Opera House and the Kennedy Center for the Performing Arts. "The first inclination of most boards and staffs is that they will save their organizations by saving money. . . . But the true turnaround artist possesses the discipline to carve out time each week to focus on artistic programming, board development, donor and press cultivation, and other activities that will make future years easier. Too many executives spend *all* of their time on short-term issues. If making this week's payroll is one's sole focus, next week is certain to be more difficult."

The same finding was reinforced by a study in the *Harvard Business Review* of how companies fared after recessions. The authors—Ranjay Gulati, Nitin Nohria, and Franz Wohlgezogen—analyzed how 4,700 public companies reacted to three global recessions. What strategy best equipped the companies to thrive after a recession?

The worst strategy was a "cut only" approach. In these companies, "pessimism permeates the organization," the authors wrote. "Centralization, strict controls, and the constant threat of more cuts build a feeling of disempowerment. The focus becomes survival—both personal and organizational."

Almost as bad was a blithe "ignore the bad news and keep

investing" strategy. With that kind of positive groupthink, "naysayers are marginalized and realities are overlooked," they found.

The best strategy? Blending cuts and investments. LESS and MORE. Just like Mollenhauer's game plan.

That balancing act is essential. If the central question of change is *How can you do something different and better?*, there are really only two answers: (1) by adding more resources; or (2) by using your resources differently.

And, for most people, option 1 is off the table. Worse still, in turnaround situations, you might need to make things "different and better" while consuming *fewer* resources, which puts even more emphasis on option 2.

Yet in change situations you will almost always need to invest *more* somewhere, because you need Resources to Restack on your Leverage Points. At Big Brothers Big Sisters, Art Mollenhauer invested in a brand-new position: the corporate partnership manager. Part of the money to fund that role came from new resources (remember his "matching grant") and part of it came from cutting back on subpar programs and staffers. Cut here, invest there.

So far in this section, we've explored three ways to muster resources: *Starting with a burst, recycling waste*, and *doing less and more*. Next we'll explore perhaps the most perennially squandered resource: motivation.

If you want to get out of a rut and leap forward, you can't do it without motivation, because motivation is the fuel for forward movement. And the good news is that motivation exists already.

The mission is to tap it.

Whirlwind review: Chapter 8, Do Less AND More

1. The third way to Restack Resources on Leverage Points is to shift them away from low-value activities. You need to simultaneously do MORE investing in your Leverage Points while investing LESS in the lower-priority activities.

2. Reallocating your resources in a new direction can be painful because of the trade-offs involved. But if you look carefully, you can minimize the sting of those trade-offs.

   a. *Rosa, the mother, chose to go to bed a bit earlier to help her stay calm in the mornings. But it was not a costless trade-off (as with waste): It meant less time in the evening with her husband.*

3. The consultancy Strategex has found that businesses consistently "over-coddle" their worst customers and "undercoddle" their best. This can be self-destructive given that the best 20% of customers might generate 150% of the profits.

   a. *As one example of this phenomenon, Strategex often finds that "on-time deliveries" are actually less common for the best customers than for the worst!*

   b. *We should consider the parallel in our personal lives: Which relation-ships are we overcoddling and undercoddling?*

4. One simple exercise—in the spirit of generating smart trade-offs—is to ask your team to fill in four quadrants: STOP, START, LESS, MORE. Note that the "STOP" and "LESS" areas are the hardest ones.

5. Restacking Resources is not just about "cutting" and it's not just about "add-ing." It's about both: less AND more at the same time.

   a. *Art Mollenhauer's turnaround of the Big Brothers Big Sisters group in Chicago hinged on his willingness to make big cuts (to programs, staff, and even board members) while also making smart investments (e.g., by funding decent office space for the beleaguered team).*

   b. *Researchers found that the best strategy for surviving a recession was blending cuts and investments. Less AND more.*

Recommendations (find live links at danheath.com/reset-links):

John J. Murphy's 2023 book, _Solution-Focused Therapy_, offers a rigorous and thorough overview of ways to get quick and lasting results with personal challenges; for an even deeper dive into solution-focused therapy tools such as bright spots and goal setting, be sure to pick up _Solution-Focused Counseling in Schools_. For more on how David Philippi applies his Pareto-inspired approach to effective leadership and family matters, check out his blog post "Dad, Son, and CEO" as well as other posts on Strategex's 80/20 paradigm. I briefly mentioned Michael Kaiser's book _The Art of the Turnaround_. ("You can't save your way to health.") It is excellent—an insider's view of how Kaiser turned around struggling and famous arts institutions such as the Royal Opera House and the Kennedy Center. A trio of researchers detail how companies have successfully weathered recessions by doing less and more in this _Harvard Business Review_ article, "Roaring Out of a Recession," which I mention in the chapter.

TAP MOTIVATION

>> You can Restack Resources on your Leverage Points
by prioritizing the work that's required <u>and</u> desired.

TAP MOTIVATION

1.

Ezra Fox was struggling to get his kids to clean up their toys. The ordinary authoritative approaches usually met a wall of resistance. One day it dawned on him: He should apply his marketing skills.

"In marketing, once I'm not interesting, the customer doesn't have to listen anymore," he said. He wondered: "Could I put a little bit of energy and craft into this in a way that might inspire them?"

He challenged them to play a game called "Hide the Evidence." The rules? *In a few minutes, your mom is going to come into the room and try to figure out what you played with. See if you can fool her by cleaning up so well that she can't figure it out.*

Shortly thereafter, the room was immaculate. And his kids loved it: *A Dad-sanctioned mission to pull one over on Mom??* The license to be sneaky was irresistible.

Ultimately, the novelty of the new approach faded, as it does with kids (and customers). So Ezra kept going back to the drawing board: a subsequent cleanup effort involved a family race, and the chance to beat Dad was as attractive as the opportunity to fool Mom.

Now, you could hear that story and think, *Oh, those were just tricks.* (If so, speaking on behalf of millions of parents, please send us more tricks.)

But attending to motivation is not a trick at all. It's the very heart of change.

To motivate people, we've got to pay attention to *their* desires. *Their* interests. *Their* hopes. And that requires empathy. Dr. Doug Eby—a senior leader at Southcentral Foundation, an Anchorage-based, Alaska Native–owned health care system—provided a great example of what this empathy could look like.

He imagined meeting with a 55-year-old male patient with diabetes—someone with a handful of young grandkids:

So I know that he is first or second generation from a particular village. He likes to hunt and fish and berry-pick and put up food for the winter. And he has young grandkids, and one of his most important life values is connecting those grandkids to their heritage. So when they grow up and become teenagers, he's going to want to help them do all those things: hunt, fish, berry-pick, and so forth. That's his goal.

In order to do that, he will need to maintain his eyesight so he can look through the scope on the rifle to kill the caribou or moose or the bear or whatever it is he's hunting. And he needs good eyesight to differentiate between ripe and unripe berries on the ground in front of him.

So we talk about diabetes and how it affects eyesight and their ability to hunt and berry-pick. And then you talk about fingertips, because you need to be able to feel the fish on the end of the line, on the fishing pole, or to pull the fish out of the net, or to use a knife or an ulu to fillet the fish or to peel the fat off the hide of what he's hunting, so you need good fingertip sensation.

And then you need good toe tip sensation because you need to walk across the tundra to go berry-picking and hunting, and you need to feel the bottom of the stream or the river, because they're all glacial fed and you can't see in the water, so you have to feel the bottom with your feet and toes.

So the goal is feet and toes, fingertips, and eyesight, preserved for 10 years from now for these four- and five-year-old grandchildren to become teenagers to hunt, fish, and berry-pick.

Now I've got him because these are the most important things in his life.

Eby is taking the time to understand the values of his patient AND to explain how those values are served by adopting healthy behaviors. Because dispensing advice is worthless unless the patient is willing to act. So Eby starts with a clear understanding of *what the patient wants*.

As the great solution-focused therapist John J. Murphy said, "You can't rearrange the furniture unless you're invited into the house."

2.

In this section of the book, we're Restacking Resources to push on the Leverage Points we've identified. In the last chapter, we focused on reallocating our resources—shifting from lower-value efforts to higher-value. Stopping some things and investing in others.

If we're looking for additional fuel for our efforts, a great place to start is with our people. The ultimate wasted resource is motivation.

It's not that motivation is *misdirected*, in the way that (say) sending the city's bulk-trash trucks up and down every block was a misdirected and wasteful use of resources. It's more like motivation is untapped energy. A sun-drenched desert with no solar panels.

Many leaders treat "change initiatives" as something to be hatched in private and then foisted on employees. When they resist, the leaders act surprised and ask, "How do I get people to buy in?"

"Buy in" is code for: How do I get people to want what I want, rather than what they want? But that's backward. If you want to get out of a rut and leap forward, go where the energy is. Tap motivation.

Assuming you've surfaced a handful of promising Leverage Points in the last section, ask yourself: Which one of those interventions would be most enthusiastically embraced by my people? It's really not more complicated than that.

In the Million Cat Challenge, Kate Hurley found that for many shelters, there was great enthusiasm for the "return to field" concept. (Which, recall, involved vaccinating and neutering/spaying cats, then releasing them back to the community.) Why? Because the shelter employees were tired of coming to work every day and killing countless cats! It was crushing. As a result, there were vast reservoirs of motivation to tap.

This kind of logic seems intuitive when it comes to externally focused work, in which you have to unite a group of partners around a common vision. You can't spark a movement if no one wants to move. But somehow the logic dissolves inside organizations. Possibly that's because we have just enough residual "command and control" mentality to think, *Nah, I shouldn't have to mess with all this "motivational" stuff. People get paid to work! That should be enough motivation for them!*

And let's be clear: You absolutely can give orders. It will often work. But even when it works, the change will come slowly and grudgingly. (Eventually, after enough pestering and threats, we all manage to watch those compliance videos and rack up the necessary continuing-ed credits.)

Let's treat you, personally, as a focus group of one: Imagine a situation at work where you have to do something you don't like and you don't agree with. And now imagine a situation where you are doing what you love and believe in. What is the difference in your effort between those two situations? What's the difference in your effectiveness?

When I ask people those questions, they don't cite modest improvement gains. (*I'm 7.3% better!*) They say they're *dramatically* more effective in the latter situation. Twice as effective, three times, even ten times. That's the incentive for us to pay attention to motivation. And that's why, when it comes to change, the shortest route between two points is not always a straight line. Because if—fueled by motivation—you can go three times as fast on the circuitous route, you'll be wise to take that one.

Tapping motivation is about finding the intersection of "what's required" and "what's desired."

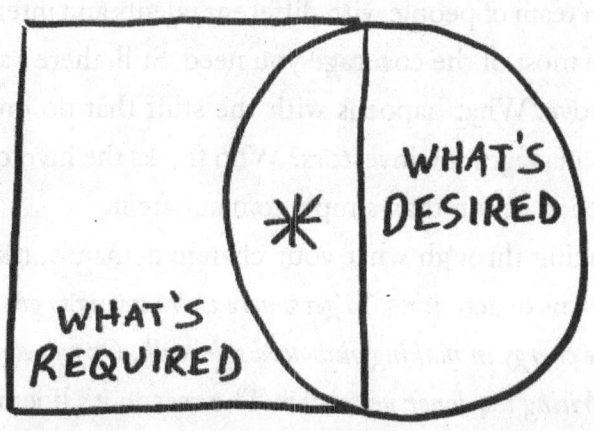

The starred area in the Venn diagram is your first move. Then again, the starred area is only a subset of the changes you need to make. So what do you do about the unclaimed area to the left? That is, what if some of the changes you need to make to succeed aren't popular?

When you're working with a team, there's not just one circle (i.e., one person's set of interests), but many:

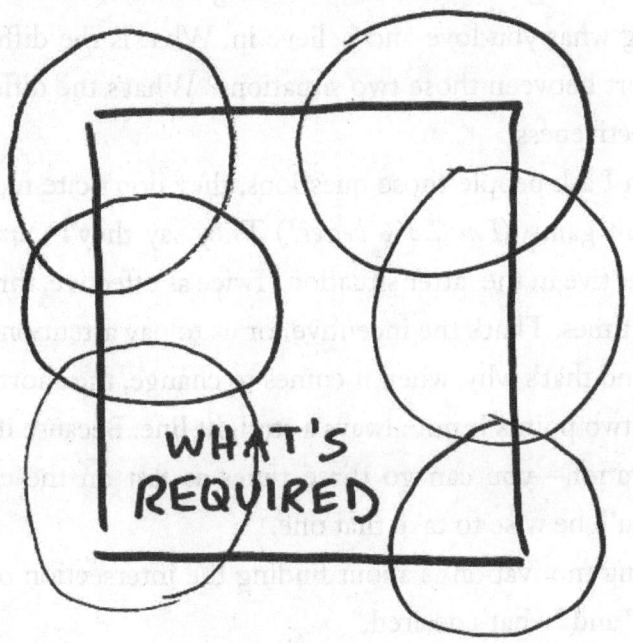

Given a team of people with different talents and interests, you'll likely have most of the coverage you need. Still, there's a gap in the picture above. What happens with the stuff that no one wants to do? (Who manages the investors? Who tracks the invoices?) Again, better to elicit action than simply to mandate it.

In thinking through what your change demands, it's helpful to think in terms of activities. *To get where we're trying to go, we'll need to invest more energy in making outbound sales calls. Or managing accounts payable. Writing the donor newsletter.* The reason it's liberating to call out these activities is that you can map them to motivations. Like organizational matchmaking.

This matching can take a surprisingly literal form. There's an idea called the "genius swap" that I learned from my friends Christine and Becky Margiotta. Christine invented the idea and Becky tried it with her team, which was leading a national campaign to get the most vulnerable homeless people off the street and into housing.

Becky's team was gathered for an offsite retreat. A rare breather. Becky asked each person on the team to grab some sticky notes. On each note, she said, write down one task that's on your plate today that you would *pay someone to take over for you*. Then, part 2: On different sticky notes, write down one task you'd be so excited to do that you'd pay for the privilege.

Next, they posted everyone's sticky notes to the wall so they could look at them together. And Becky said it was magical. Because you could see, right in front of you, that there were a bunch of matches.

One person's "pay to get rid of" activities corresponded exactly to someone else's "pay to take it on" activities. One person hated budgeting. Another pined for it.

Becky herself scored a match. Fatigued from traveling, she was eager to offload the need to speak at regional meetings and conferences, a critical way of attracting interest in the campaign. Meanwhile, one of her colleagues, Linda, was chomping at the bit to do more traveling and speaking.

So they just swapped.

Not everything was neatly swappable, of course. But Becky said that, for her, the swaps were only a small part of the value. Consider the list of activities that people said they'd pay to take on. Becky's attitude was: Everything on that list is a yes. *Yes, you can do that.* If people were that excited about something, she figured they would invest the energy to do it well, and the organization would benefit.

Meanwhile, for the "pay to get rid of" activities that didn't find a match, she'd promise the team to work on them. Were those tasks really necessary? In the spirit of chapter 7, could they be "shifted right"? Or, when they had the funding for another employee, could they bundle up the unloved activities and hire someone who adored them?

That's how you unleash motivation.

Now, I do want to acknowledge that for many HR and legal employees, the above paragraphs may have triggered a seizure. In large organizations, this kind of shape-shifting can be complicated. (For small organizations, by contrast, I refuse to believe that you shouldn't run a genius swap every year for the rest of time.)

There *is* value in standardizing roles. It's nice when employees can shift from one plant to another, or one region to another, and still fit in smoothly, because the roles are the same.

But we sometimes act as though an employee's highest calling is to stay safely within the bullet points of their job description. The reality, though, is that when we don't tap motivation, we squander it. It's like a hydropower project that runs on the flows from garden hoses—predictable and controllable—while ignoring the massive (and messier) waterfall nearby.

3.

When you're struggling to propel yourself forward, your best move is to harness the waterfall. That was what Dianne Connery learned in Pottsboro, Texas, a town of about 2,500 people, 75 miles north of Dallas, up near the Oklahoma border. "Some small towns have a beautiful little courthouse, that kind of thing," said Connery. "This is a poor small town. It's not modern. It's not quaint. It's rusted metal buildings."

In 2010, Connery—cajoled by a friend—began attending the Pottsboro Library board meetings. The library had roughly the same charm as the town. Housed in the former post office, it was a 3,600-square-foot box stocked full of dusty old pulp novels that no one read. Chronically understaffed (with volunteers only) and underfunded, its future looked hopeless.

"When I got involved, we were preparing to shut down," said Connery in a public talk. "Every board meeting was just this discussion of: How much money do we have left? How many more months can we keep going until we have to close? . . . They were such a downer."

New ideas tended to be greeted with an enthusiastic smothering. At one point, a board member wondered whether the library's meeting room could be offered for free to community groups. That way, at least people would be *coming in and out of the building*. It would be a start.

That suggestion launched a series of discussions about the rules and policies that should govern such usage, and the importance of posting those rules publicly, and the need for each group using the meeting space to provide a written attestation that they would abide by the full set of rules, one of those rules being that under no circumstances should people bring shrimp to their meetings, because one time long ago somebody had let shrimp tails slip down the drain and they ended up stinking up the place so badly that it was deemed crucial to ban the species from the premises.

Connery called this the Shrimp Tail Doctrine: a misguided obsession with rules and policies at the expense of the bigger picture—that bigger picture being that the library was dying, barring a radical rejuvenation.

Feeling there was little to lose, Connery agreed to take over the library as a volunteer. Her leadership strategy was inspired by a *Seinfeld* episode called "The Opposite." In one scene, George Costanza, sitting in a diner with Jerry and Elaine, is bemoaning his life choices:

GEORGE COSTANZA: It became very clear to me sitting out there today, that every decision I've ever made, in my entire life, has been wrong. My life is the complete opposite of everything I want it to be. Every instinct I have, in every aspect of life, be it something to wear, something to eat . . . It's all been wrong.

. . .

JERRY SEINFELD: If every instinct you have is wrong, then the opposite would have to be right.

GEORGE COSTANZA: Yes, I will do the opposite. I used to sit here and do nothing, and regret it for the rest of the day, so now I will do the opposite, and I will do something! . . . [Inspired, George gets up and approaches an attractive woman sitting at the counter.] My name is George. I'm unemployed and I live with my parents.

ATTRACTIVE WOMAN: I'm Victoria. Hi.

Connery, channeling George Costanza, decided to do the opposite of almost everything the library had been doing. She abandoned the Shrimp Tail Doctrine: "What if we find ways to encourage people to come and then . . . figure it out?"

"It was obvious to me that we needed to reach people who never use the library," Connery said. "We had to fight the preconception of what a library offers."

What followed was an explosion of activities, attractions, and outreach. Like cooking classes on how to feed a family on a tight budget. A "library of things" where patrons could check out canning supplies, bicycles, sewing machines, or a power washer. A Friday-night "Cocktails & Coloring" fundraiser, which featured adult coloring books and drinks from a new distillery in a nearby town.

To make room for more of these programs, she did what some library die-hards considered sacrilege: She brought in a tractor-trailer to get rid of thousands of books—romance novels, outdated encyclopedias, and more—that no one had checked out in 10 years or more.

The new library was about saying "yes": harnessing the enthusiasm of community members. That's the waterfall approach—find the natural energy and channel it to do work. "People will volunteer and get excited about things that are meaningful to them," Connery said.

She told Pottsboro citizens: "Fit in where your passion is. If you have an interest in something, go for it. And I'm not going to micromanage it."

Not everything worked. A much-hyped movie night drew an underwhelming 10 people. A community garden, which had received a burst of initial caretaking, eventually withered from inattention. But other initiatives drew audiences who had never been library patrons before: Teens flocked to play esports. Seniors came in to learn to use tablet computers or to get their wills notarized. A telemedicine program—for which the library eventually became an exemplar—brought in community members who needed health care.

And sometimes they just did things for the sheer joy of doing them: Just before the library replaced its aging carpet, the staff brought in a pair of miniature horses for a summer event. (Because if you're gonna trash the carpets, why not *really* trash the carpets?)

The place was packed wall-to-wall with kids, all gaga for the furry guests.

The local newspaper covered the scene, featuring this photo that would make David Lynch smile:

(I can't help thinking that, at some subconscious level perhaps, the miniature-horse visit was orchestrated specifically to torment the Shrimp Tail people.)

Now, granted, there is a kitchen-sink energy to these experiments. The library went from trying nothing to trying everything.

But the efforts weren't random. Underlying the efforts was a clear and simple strategy: Connery believed that the library could not survive without ongoing government support. And that support had to be earned: The library had to convince taxpayers that it was worth the investment. The Leverage Point was: citizens getting increasingly attached to the place.

"What will make this place so important to the community that there would be rioting in the streets if we had to close?" said Connery in her public talk.

The rioting proved unnecessary because the strategy worked. More and more people came to the library, more and more often. It became a social hub.

Since 2011, it has effectively been enshrined in the town budget, which saved it from the brink of financial collapse.

Librarians from around the country started paying attention to the Pottsboro story, because in a time when many libraries were struggling, here was a small institution in a small town in Texas with nothing going for it—no endowment, no snazzy building, no special collections—that remade itself to suit the needs of its community. A library that made itself indispensable by tapping motivation.

4.

To reset your efforts, you need to tap motivation, just as Connery did in Pottsboro. Sometimes, though, the initial enthusiasm for change can be fleeting. To stay in motion—to keep pushing forward—requires you to *sustain* motivation. And one of the best tools for sustaining motivation is recognition.

"You get what you celebrate," said Frank Blake, the former CEO of Home Depot.

After Blake became CEO in 2007, he stressed five specific areas for improvement, the most important of which was customer service. He wanted associates to feel empowered to take care of customers. But Home Depot had *hundreds of thousands* of employees. It was hard to break through with a message.

Most executives in this situation seem to instinctively lob bland bromides: *At Home Depot, we take pride in standing behind you, our trusted employees, as empowered agents of empowerment.* But Blake took a different approach. "No one gives a rat's ass what your memo says," he said.

At one point, Blake had the chance to speak to about 3,000 store managers, and he used that forum to retell a story he'd heard. At a Home Depot store in north Georgia, a customer—an older gentleman—was checking out with a cartload of lumber. The cashier asked him whether he'd found everything he needed. He said he had. Then, making conversation, she asked what project he was working on.

The man paused. Then he replied that his grandson had passed away, and he had decided to build the coffin with his own hands.

The cashier immediately replied: "Please, sir, don't even think of paying," and waved him through the line.

When Blake shared that story with his store managers, he said, "You could have heard a pin drop."

Why did Blake share that particular story? It was certainly memorable—surprising and moving. And the cashier who was praised must have felt good about the recognition. But Blake's actual goal was to conjure a vision and motivate his team to achieve it. He was saying, implicitly, *Here's what it means to deliver amazing customer service. In this case, it meant giving away our products for free! This cashier didn't ask the boss for permission—she just did it. And not only is that okay with me, I'm going out of my way to praise this woman in front of all of you.*

Blake became a zealot for the power of recognition. When managers would approach him for more resources, he'd say, "Don't talk to me about your resource allocation until you've told me you've burned all your free fuel." When they asked what he meant by "free fuel," he'd say, "Your free fuel is praise and recognition. You come in and tell me how you're praising and recognizing your people to get where we need to go. And then we'll talk about resources."

Blake didn't just talk about recognition, he modeled it. He was known for sending handwritten notes to employees thanking them—with specific details—for things they had done. He spent every Sunday afternoon writing those notes, and he wrote *thousands* of them.

Here's the CEO of a Fortune 50 company, devoting part of every weekend to celebrating his people. That's how powerfully he believed in recognition.

As you make progress toward your new goal, make sure that *what you celebrate* is aligned with *where you're headed*. "You've got to figure out what you need and celebrate the people who lead the way," Blake said.

5.

As much as I believe in everything positive and constructive that has preceded this sentence, I also believe that there is a countervailing truth of human nature: Where there is change, there is resistance. No matter how enlightened your methods, there will be people on your team who will dig in their heels. (There was surely one person in the ballroom listening to Frank Blake's talk who, after hearing the story about the grandfather building his grandson's coffin, thought to himself, *This is ridiculous. That guy shoulda paid for the wood!*) What do you do about the resisters in your midst?

Let's break down some numbers for a moment. For any particular change goal, there will always be people who are with you from the start. Let's say 20%. (If there's literally no one who's with you,

you have the wrong change goal. Full stop.) There will be a larger group (~60%) in the middle who are indifferent or swayable. And the remainder (~20%) will be against you.*

For the resisters, let's recall a Ken Davis (Gartner) quote from chapter 3: "If you want change you've either got to change the people . . . or change the people." The latter is always an option: It's painful to let people go, but don't forget it's also painful for everyone else to deal with the constant negativity and foot-dragging. (There's no "pain-free" option, in other words.) For now, though, let's assume that letting people go is a last resort and focus instead on ways to improve your odds with the current team intact.

Here are three thoughts to guide your work: First, don't make the mistake of accepting these 20/60/20 numbers as inevitable. Might there be another Leverage Point where the numbers would be more favorable? What if there's another Leverage Point, perhaps slightly less attractive in pure strategic terms, that would attract 80% enthusiasts instead of 20%? Well, do that first! Go where the energy is.

Second, if there's not a better Leverage Point, then could you barter with the middle 60% and the resistant 20% to make the change more exciting? Maybe there are some problems or irritants that you could resolve for them. *If you'll help me with this, I'll help you with that.* (Remember how, in the hospital receiving area story that began the book, the leader canvassed the employees for nuisances he could fix, like the erratic cart wheels.) Or could you reconfigure their responsibilities to add some appeal? In other words, even if the change as a whole is unmotivating to them, could they take

---

*These numbers are made up, of course, but I've heard these exact numbers—20/60/20—from enough different leaders that I've come to believe there must be some folk wisdom behind them.

charge of some aspects that are more in keeping with their interests, à la the genius swap?

Finally, how could you tap the energy of your pro-change faction to score some quick wins? Because visible progress changes minds. (Tapping the sign again: "Of all the things that can boost emotions, motivation, and perceptions during a workday, the single most important is making progress in meaningful work.")

No one in the hospital receiving area was hungrily awaiting the chance to reinvent the way they worked. Their enthusiasm had to be earned. And it was earned by showing them that their effort would bear fruit. That it would make their lives less stressful. And, most important, that it would help the people they served—the doctors and nurses waiting to receive time-sensitive supplies. ("An empty room is a beautiful thing, man.")

Our goal is to tap motivation to yield progress, and then use the evidence of that progress to motivate others, whose kindled enthusiasm can then be tapped for still more energy. That cycle can fuel your forward movement.

Progress is the spark that makes believers of skeptics.

Whirlwind review: Chapter 9, Tap Motivation

1. The fourth way to Restack Resources on Leverage Points is to harness motivation. Think of it like a sun-drenched desert with no solar panels. It could provide valuable energy—but only if it's tapped.

2. If you want to fuel change, pay attention to what your constituents want, considering their interests and desires.

   a. *Ezra Fox's "hide the evidence" idea tapped his kids' natural interest in games (as opposed to trying to convince them to be interested in cleaning).*

   b. *Dr. Doug Eby explained to his diabetic patient why better self-care would honor the most important things in his life—his desire to hunt and fish with his grandkids.*

3. Tapping motivation is about finding the intersection of "what's required" and "what's desired." (Remember the Venn diagram illustrating that.)

4. Your teammates will have different interests. How can you ensure that those interests can be channeled toward "what's required"? Consider a "genius swap": the idea that you can simply trade responsibilities according to interest.

   a. *Becky Margiotta and her team found some easy swaps to make. (Becky traded her public speaking to Linda.) More broadly, the exercise helped surface where people's individual passions lay.*

5. To Restack Resources on your Leverage Points, don't think "How do I get buy-in for my idea?" Think, instead, "How could I harness the waterfall of available motivation to propel a new effort?"

   a. *Dianne Connery revived the dying Pottsboro Library by finding pockets of passion that could be yoked to the mission of the library. Ultimately, she made the library indispensable to the community.*

6. How do you handle change skeptics? Try: (1) picking a Leverage Point with more enthusiasts and fewer skeptics; (2) bargaining with the lukewarm or resistant factions; and/or (3) tapping the motivation of believers to make progress, and then count on those visible results to change minds.

7. Progress is the spark that makes believers of skeptics.

Recommendations (find live links at <u>danheath.com/reset-links</u>):

On the theme of "progress making believers of skeptics," I want to return to the source I cited in the introduction: Teresa Amabile and Steven Kramer's insightful book _The Progress Principle_. As a reminder, they found that making progress was the #1 motivator of employees. For a great primer on their research, check out Amabile's Talks at Google <u>presentation</u>. Dr. Doug Eby, the Southcentral Foundation's Executive Vice President of Specialty Services, offers a look into their radically different approach to primary care in this talk about the Nuka Model (<u>part 1</u>, Eby starts at 6:15, and <u>part 2</u>). I find Southcentral's approach inspiring—if only more health systems would follow in their footsteps. For more on how Dianne Connery started tapping into her community to resuscitate and transform the Pottsboro Library, check out her inspiring presentation from 2016, "<u>Flip the Script: Changing the Direction of the Library</u>." Finally, a great all-purpose resource on motivation is Dan Pink's book _Drive_.

10

LET PEOPLE DRIVE

>> You can Restack Resources on
your Leverage Points by giving your team
the autonomy to own the change effort.

LET PEOPLE DRIVE

1.

When patients' kidneys fail, they must undergo dialysis, a procedure where a machine (the dialyzer) filters their blood, acting as artificial kidneys. Dialysis can be a grueling process—patients might have to visit a center for three 4-hour sessions every week. Attached to a machine. Sitting quietly in a hushed environment, with too much time to think. And barring a transplant, patients with kidney failure will continue on dialysis for the rest of their lives.

Richard Gibney, an experienced nephrologist (kidney doctor) based in Waco, Texas, had assumed that was the way dialysis would always be. A necessary evil. Then he attended a conference where a speaker told the story of Christian Farman, a young Swedish man who had asked to take over his own dialysis.* A nurse, Britt-Mari

*The speaker was Maureen Bisognano from the Institute for Healthcare Improvement (IHI). A shout-out to the IHI, which I have found to be a consistent source of inspiration over the years and across many books. They do excellent quality-improvement work in health care, and I'd strongly encourage any reader in the health care industry to get involved with them—read their newsletters, attend their conferences, etc.

Banck, agreed to train him, and within five weeks, he was mostly self-sufficient.

Farman's clinic, inspired by his example, started offering self-dialysis to other patients, and the practice spread quickly. Not only were patients *able* to handle the technical side of the work, they seemed to thrive as a result.

In control of their care, they reshaped that dull dialysis time. Some of them actually exercised during their self-treatments—riding stationary bikes or lifting weights.

Gibney, amazed and excited, returned to his clinic, evangelizing for self-care dialysis. "My team thought I was crazy," he wrote online. Trying to convince his colleagues that the idea wasn't ludicrous, he actually flew over Christian Farman and Banck from Sweden to Waco.

Gibney remembers their visit:

> They began by politely asking questions: Would you be willing to turn the dialysis machine to face the patients? Would you give patients permission to touch the machines? Would you let patients insert the needles into their own bodies?
>
> These inquiries represented the diametric opposite of our practice at the time. Up until then, we pretty much told patients to sit down, put out your arm, be quiet, and don't touch anything. (We were polite, but that was essentially our protocol.) Much as I hate to admit it now, our treatment encouraged boredom, depression, and learned helplessness.

Some of Gibney's colleagues were open to the idea but had reservations about it. Merry Smith, a nurse, wondered whether patients would be capable of shouldering the work. Sometimes even the patients' own family members were skeptical.

But Smith was surprised by how many patients volunteered for self-care. As a result, her own role shifted: She became a coach as well as a caregiver. She'd tell the patients, "You're gonna watch me do this, and then you're gonna do it."

But it wasn't just one-way communication. The self-care patients started catching mistakes: the wrong dose of heparin, or the wrong set of lines. Gibney said that the dialysis centers started to feel more collegial and collaborative. Less like an assembly line.

Gibney and his staff were *letting the patients drive*. To "let people drive" is to give them autonomy—the freedom to manage their own work. Gibney often repeated a quote from Warner Slack: "The least utilized resource in medicine is the patient."

This isn't an argument for total freedom. Autonomy is not *always* better—it's possible to go too far, as we'll see. But the benefits of letting people drive are profound. So profound, in fact, that it's hard to imagine a high-functioning team that lacks a strong measure of autonomy.

Gibney's clinic experienced these benefits. When people from other dialysis centers came to visit—self-care dialysis was still very much a novelty—they were shocked. "They'd say, 'This is unbelievable,'" recalled Gibney. "'We've never seen a happy dialysis unit.'"

Eugene Payne, a 62-year-old from Canton, Michigan, learned the ins and outs of self-care dialysis from watching YouTube videos, including Gibney's. Being mechanically inclined, he was motivated to take more control of the process. He was the first person in his facility to ask for self-care.

For him, the payoff was immense. "It's a reward that I just can't explain," he said. "I'm not letting my illness hold me back. I look forward to doing it—I'm not depressed about dialysis."

Patients like Payne were extremely conscientious about the

procedure, for obvious reasons: "When I look at the machine, that's my life," Payne said. "That is what's keeping me alive."

Perhaps because of this extra caution, it wasn't just the patient experience that improved from self-care dialysis, it was the medical outcomes, too. At Gibney's clinic, a year after launching the experiment, the self-care patients were experiencing fewer emergencies: Only 0.7 hospitalizations per patient, compared to 1.9 per patient for traditional dialysis.

Smith, the nurse, said that the embrace of self-care dialysis had changed her: "It opened my eyes, my heart to the fact that people are amazing and capable of a lot, even in the most scary and overwhelming circumstances," she said. "And if you believe in them and give them permission, they will rise."

2.

Letting people drive is naturally motivating. In that sense, granting autonomy is a continuation of the themes of the previous chapter (*Tap motivation*). But letting people drive has a second advantage that is less intuitive. It's something we'll discover in the story of Guy Krueger.

A fraction of an inch shifted Krueger's fate. In 2008, Krueger was competing in the trials for a spot on the US Olympic archery team. It came down to the last attempt. The arrows flew, and Krueger's was judged barely out, his rival's barely in. And that was it—his Olympic dream was over.

Krueger decided it was time for him to switch to coaching, and he took a role at the Olympic Training Center. "Basically in a span of three weeks, I went from competing against these athletes to coaching and having some type of leadership role over them," he said. "Not a super-successful transition."

Unsuccessful because Krueger tried to coach athletes in the same semiauthoritarian way he'd been coached himself. "I tried to be really direct, like 'Here's the information, take it or leave it,'" he said. Then, he admitted, "Well, actually, not even 'take it or leave it.' It was just, 'Do this.'"

A few years later, it was time to prepare for the 2012 Olympics. By tradition, the athletes got to select the two coaches who would travel with them to the Olympic Games. "I just knew that they would select me," he said. There were only two coaches who worked with the athletes daily. Two coaches, two slots, simple math.

But they didn't pick him. Instead of Krueger, they chose another coach, one who helped out less frequently. Krueger was shocked. He would miss the Olympics for a second time.

A year later his health deteriorated. He sustained a "pretty horrific back injury" and was bedridden for several months before surgery. During this miserable time, not one athlete called or visited or texted to see how he was doing.

"When the people that you're working with day in and day out—and like 60 hours a week at that time—don't notice that you're not there, or reach out, it's pretty eye-opening," he said.

It was a painful wake-up call. After successful surgery got him back on his feet, he enrolled himself in a training program for coaches. He wanted help.

His conversion moment came when he was exposed to the work of the sports scientist Gabriele Wulf and her approach to harnessing the focus and motivation of athletes.

Coaches shouldn't act like a boss and tell athletes what to do, she advised. They should elicit. They should guide. Specifically, a coach should push athletes' focus outward and channel their own desires as the force of improvement. Because the coach can't shoot the arrows for them. The coach should let the athletes drive.

Krueger saw the wisdom of that approach immediately. From the training, he learned to give feedback differently. Traditionally, archery coaches had been hyperfocused on muscle movements: *Set your hand at this angle. Grip the bow like this. Keep your tricep tight. Squeeze your back together.*

Even for experienced athletes, though, that advice could be paralyzing: *Am I really doing it right? Is my tricep "tight"?? What if the muscle movements look right from the outside but are not right internally?*

Channeling Wulf's advice, Krueger turned athletes' focus outward, away from their muscles. Now he'd tell an athlete, *Imagine the sleeve of your shirt moving back behind you.* Or, *Shoot the arrow through the target, not just to it.* Notice that this language gives direction but allows for adaptation—different athletes can respond to the prompts in different ways, using different muscle patterns, while still succeeding. (Wulf calls this technique "external focus.")*

A more profound shift for Kruger was abandoning the practice of giving direct instruction to athletes. Now, Krueger elicits goals from athletes and helps them get what they want. Here's a sample conversation he modeled to illustrate the process:

KRUEGER: What do you want to focus on today?

ARCHER: I want to focus on my mental process.

---

*Learning about Wulf's work struck a nostalgic chord with me, because it reminded me of my junior high school football coach. I can only remember three things he said. Two of them, I realized, were external-focus cues. In the weight room, he'd tell us to "hug the log" when we were doing dumbbell flies. For barbell squats, he'd tell us to "push through the floor." Classic external focus! He was way ahead of his time! By the way, for completeness, the third thing I remember him saying was "You're doggin' it, Heath!" Which was rude but fair.

KRUEGER: Okay, run me through it—what does that normally look like?

ARCHER: [describes it]

KRUEGER: Okay, now do a shot for me so I can see what that looks like in real time as you're running that through your head.

The ARCHER prepares and takes a shot.

KRUEGER: All right, can you rate that on a 1 to 10 scale of how good it was, with 10 being where you want to be?

ARCHER: Oh, that was a 5.

KRUEGER: What would it take for it to be an 8?

ARCHER: Well, I need to do X, Y, and Z.

KRUEGER: Okay, let's see if you can do those things this time.

This coaching is flipped. Instead of pushing ideas onto the athletes, Krueger pulls ideas from them. They set the goals, he doesn't. They provide the assessment, he doesn't.

Krueger was transformed as a coach. Now he let athletes take the lead, and it didn't take long for him to rebuild their trust in him. "I remember one of the athletes said one day: 'I don't know what you're doing differently, but we like it,'" said Krueger.*

---

*These are Olympic-caliber athletes, of course, which means they are very capable of "driving." You couldn't very well start a kid's first guitar lesson with the prompt "So, what do you want to focus on today?" Beginners will obviously need more direction. BUT even in these "beginner" situations, it is crazy not to pay attention to their motivation! If a kid wants to learn how to play "Yesterday," then that's the fuel the teacher needs to sustain their interest and practice.

In early 2015, he was named the Women's Head Coach for USA Archery. By October 2015, the women's team was ranked 2nd in the world (up from 18th the year prior). It was the team's highest world ranking ever.

Meanwhile, Krueger was so excited about what he'd learned that he eventually stopped training archers and started training other coaches. He now serves as the Director of Education at USA Archery.

3.

In situations where we want to see quick improvement, we often have the instinct to take more control. We grab the wheel ourselves. *I'll just take over. I'll just tell them what to do.* But that's exactly the wrong approach, because we need people's investment and their energy. That was the lesson Krueger learned.

But let's look at his story through another lens. When Krueger was micromanaging the athletes, he was expending a lot of energy that was not valued by the "customer" (the athlete). The instruction was both unwanted and ineffective. What does that sound like?

Yep, waste. And this is the second part of the justification for letting people drive—it both *boosts motivation* and *reduces waste*. It cuts waste by reducing micromanagement. Recall that another form of waste is "Nonutilized talent." As you read in chapter 7, "It's wasteful when people are playing below their level."

Autonomy helps people operate at the top of their range. When you're in charge of something, you act with more conscientiousness—and tap more of your skills—than if you're a cog in the machine. With self-dialysis, the patient becomes an active contributor, rather than a passive recipient of care.

Note that autonomy is not miracle dust—it's not an unbounded positive. (If all employees could do whatever they wanted at any given time, one fears that the very institution of staff meetings could crumble and fall.) It's not even clear that employees *want* unlimited freedom themselves. Years ago, I did a survey asking people to describe the best and worst jobs they'd had in their lives. One consistent theme in the worst jobs was feeling disempowered.

Here's one person: "I felt like I was wasting my time and energy. . . . I started doing less because it was easier on my ego than creating work that was crushed. . . . I learned to do exactly what [the boss] asked and nothing more so pretty much I was an extension of his work which didn't make me feel valued at all." In other words, this person not only wasn't allowed to drive—they were practically locked in the trunk.

But, interestingly, almost no one said that their best job was when they had complete autonomy. Many people, reflecting on their best jobs, remarked that they had a clear understanding of what was expected of them. They were supported in their roles. They were mentored.

That's not a cry to be left alone! People do want to drive. But they also want guardrails and a safety net if something goes wrong. So ultimately, it seems, the desire is for bounded autonomy.

How do you manage that tension between "fewer constraints" and "more support"? One inspiration comes from Spotify, the company behind the music- and audio-streaming app. In a great video describing Spotify's engineering culture, the coach and consultant Henrik Kniberg highlights the concepts of autonomy and alignment. He points out that, at first glance, these concepts seem like they're two different ends of the same scale:

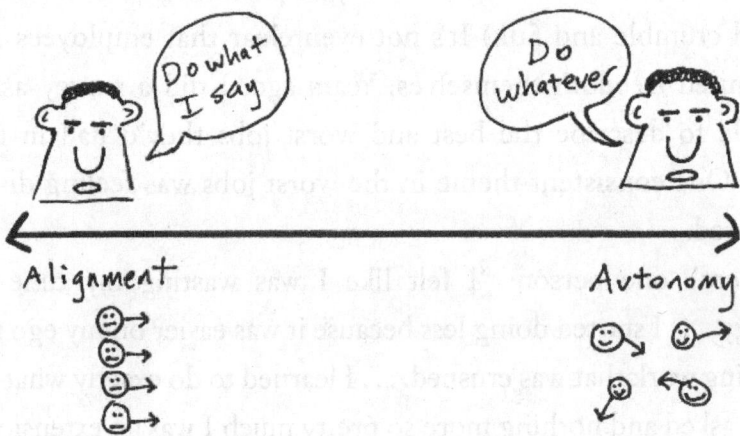

Illustrations adapted from Henrik Kniberg's video "Spotify Engineering Culture"

But, Kniberg said, Spotify thinks of these as two independent dimensions. (And, reader, no business book is complete until you have seen a 2×2 matrix. Here is yours.)

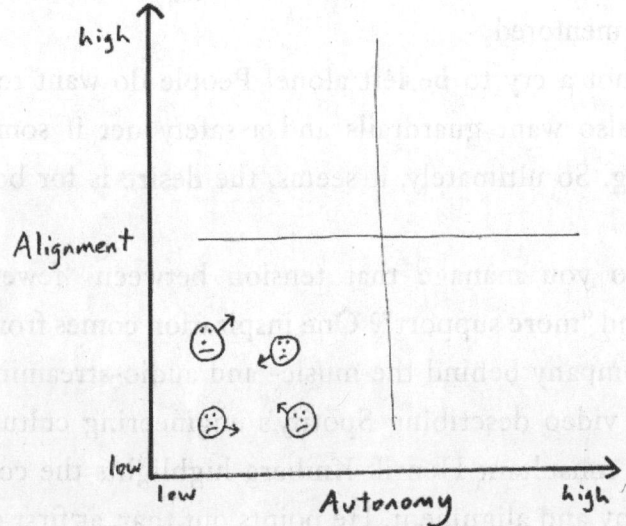

With low autonomy and low alignment, as shown above, it's a micromanagement culture. *Just be quiet and do what I say.* (Ken Blanchard said, "The opposite of trust is not distrust—it's control.")

One square up from that, you've still got low autonomy but better alignment:

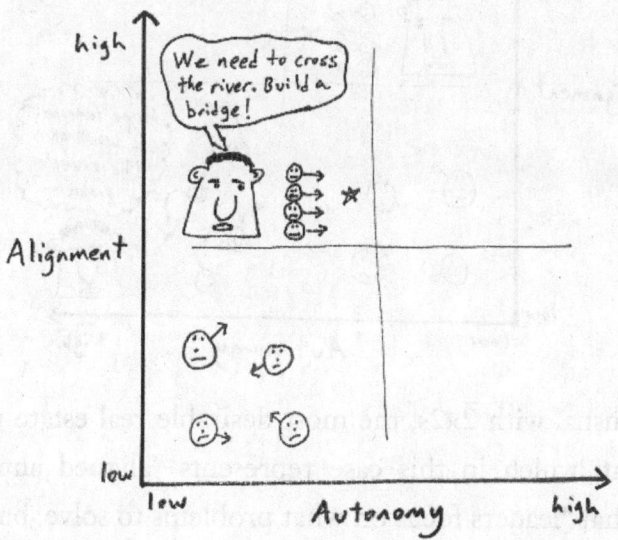

In that upper left square, Kniberg says, "leaders are good at communicating what problem needs to be solved, but they're also telling people how to solve it." That's the way Guy Krueger, the archery coach, originally taught his athletes: *Do this, do that.*

The bottom right—high autonomy but low alignment—means "teams do whatever they want and basically all run in different directions. Leaders are helpless and our product becomes a Frankenstein." That looks like this:

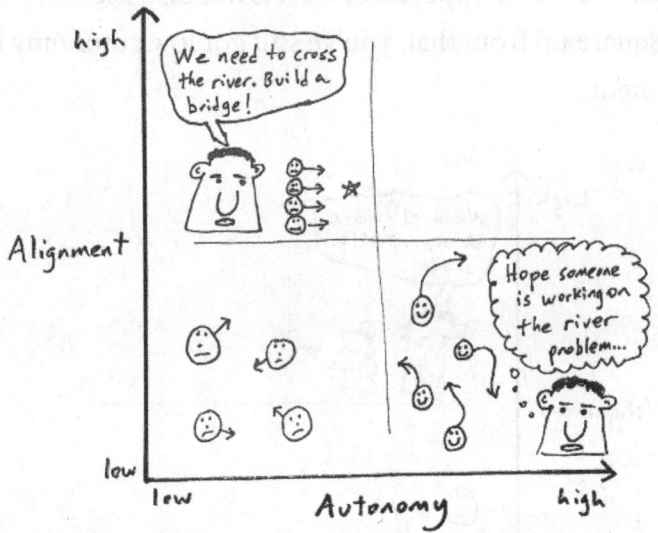

As per usual with 2×2s, the most desirable real estate is in the upper right, which in this case represents "aligned autonomy." Meaning that "leaders focus on what problems to solve, but let the teams figure out how to solve it. . . . The stronger alignment we have, the more autonomy we can afford to grant," Kniberg said. Here's aligned autonomy:

Management says, "We need to cross the river—figure out how!"* That's aligned autonomy.

It's Spotify's approach. It's Guy Krueger's approach. It's the self-dialysis clinic's approach. And, if we want to bring the maximum force to bear as we Restack Resources, it should be our approach as well.

4.

One interesting dilemma is: How do you move between locations in the 2×2? If you're stuck in one of the low-autonomy squares, could you ever shift to the upper right (high alignment, high autonomy)?

That ambitious shift was proposed at T-Mobile in 2015 by a leader named Callie Field. As executive vice president of customer care, Field was in charge of the company's call centers, and up until that point, T-Mobile's call centers had been managed as so-called cost centers. Meaning that the less spent to operate them, the better. (*Why invest lavishly in something that doesn't bring in money?* Or so the logic goes.)

When you have this cost-center mindset, you have a perverse incentive to try to deter customers from calling you. So you bury the 1-800 number. Redirect people to self-service tools. Make people wait when they call, knowing some of them will give up. And for those who persevere, you train your call-center reps to rush them off the phone as quickly as possible.

---

*An even better approach (riffing on the themes from the last chapter on *tapping motivation*) would be if management said: "To finish our mission, we could either climb the steep hill or cross the river. Pick whichever one you're more excited about and then figure out how."

Field proposed a radical rethink. What if customer support wasn't managed as a drain on business but as a way to cultivate business? (*Consider the goal of the goal.*) She proposed a "dedicated team" model for T-Mobile's customers. It was called "Team of Experts," or TEX. The 47-person teams would be organized by geography. One specific team at T-Mobile might be responsible for, say, 120,000 customers in Detroit. The reps on that team would no longer receive a random cross section of calls every day. Instead, every single call they fielded would be from Detroit. And everyone sitting around them would also be taking calls from Detroit.

The redesign was inspired by support operations in B2B companies, in which each client might have a dedicated team to assist them. Over time, that team would get to know the client well. That knowledge would lead to better service. The relationship would deepen.

"In the end, we had a simple goal: customer happiness," Field told Matthew Dixon, who wrote about T-Mobile for *Harvard Business Review*. (The story here draws heavily on Dixon's account.) "We figured happy customers would stay longer, spend more with us, and recommend us to others."

In the TEX model, their incentives would be different, too. Most call centers focused on minimizing call time. But the TEX teams had different priorities: Retaining customers. Growing their business. Reducing their calls—not by making it harder for them to call, but by solving issues on the first try.

So, to get back to the Spotify 2×2, what T-Mobile was proposing was a vault from the lower-left square to the upper-right. Before, the call-center reps acted as solo agents, receiving a never-ending stream of random calls—monitored and micromanaged throughout the day. After the shift to TEX, though, they'd be part of a team given the autonomy to manage a specific set of customers with certain clear goals in mind. Autonomy plus alignment.

This was audacious thinking. And there were plenty of TEX skeptics even within T-Mobile. "I can't tell you how many people were running around thinking that we were going to totally blow up the cost structure," said Jon Freier, president of the consumer group. "Hundreds of millions of dollars are going to be added into the cost structure, and this is going to be a complete and colossal failure."

The cost worries were real. Field and Freier knew that TEX would require an enormous up-front investment. Worse, they knew that the model would make the call center less efficient. The "average call time"—a critical metric in most call centers—would increase. Not temporarily, but forever. Because building relationships takes longer.

The dedicated-support model had worked in B2B, which gave them some faith. But B2B support operations are comparatively low volume. If you support a small number of major clients, you can get to know them pretty well. With TEX, though, the teams would deal with huge populations. Even the bubbliest extrovert couldn't hope to "get to know" 120,000 people in Detroit. Would knowledge of the area—not the client—be sufficient to provide better service?

Ultimately, they made the bet and spent the millions to bring TEX to life. The call centers were redesigned so that everyone on a TEX team could sit together. The team members serving Detroit, for instance, sat together in Chattanooga. They decorated their area with "Motor City" signage and pennants from the Detroit Tigers and Pistons.

A rep in Idaho who served San Diego told Dixon, "We're constantly talking about what's happening there. I've never been to San Diego, but I know what's going on in the local news, where the best place is for fish tacos, and what the surf report looks like for the next few days."

As hoped, the TEX model made the reps more responsive to customers. When a brush fire caused an outage in San Diego, T-Mobile customers started calling to complain. In the old model, a rep unfamiliar with the situation would have apologized generically. Promised to file a report with engineering.

With TEX, though, the team knew what was happening, because they were talking to each other throughout the day. The rep could reply immediately, "Yes, we are tracking the fire, and we've spoken with the engineers on the ground, and they are estimating that service will return within 24 hours."

The model was remarkably successful. By the first quarter of 2018, TEX had scored a rare triple win for company, customers, and employees. For T-Mobile, the cost to serve customers was down by 13% from 2016. This was driven by a 21% reduction in calls per account. Getting things right the first time worked.

For customers, the model made support easier. Transferred calls were way down. And they appreciated the team's familiarity with their area—net promoter score jumped from 43% to 67%.

Best of all, employees felt like less of a cog in the TEX model. It offered autonomy and camaraderie. As a result, absenteeism dropped 24% and staff turnover plunged from 42% annually to 22%. (Those are eye-popping numbers for a customer service environment.)

The success of the TEX model provides us a nice opportunity to review the lessons of the Restack Resources section. T-Mobile's leaders had a goal: "customer happiness," as Callie Field said. And they'd identified a Leverage Point (better service as a driver of happiness) in pursuit of that goal.

So how did they Restack Resources on that Leverage Point?

First, they *recycled waste* by trying to eliminate a customer's need to place a second or third call to get issues resolved. By handling problems on the first call—even if that first contact took a bit longer—a lot of wasteful activity was prevented.

Second, as we've stressed in this chapter, they *let people drive*. The very heart of the TEX model, after all, was to give call center employees more ownership over their work. That autonomy fueled progress.

Third, and this anticipates the final part of the Restack Resources section, the TEX teams benefited from quicker learning. As an example, a team covering Salt Lake City noticed that many young people were calling to cancel their accounts. Together, the team members pieced together the story: Young Mormons were preparing to leave on their two-year missions. At that time, they were forbidden to bring phones. But following a bit of legwork, the team discovered that the young missionaries could bring tablets.

Now, when those young Mormons called to cancel, the T-Mobile reps simply offered to switch their service to a tablet—and even offered to provide the tablet for free. That helped the missionaries, and it helped T-Mobile.

Notice that in a traditional call center, this insight would have stayed buried. A large call center might employ tens of thousands of people. In that context, even if 10 different young missionaries called to cancel their phones on the same day, no one would notice. The numbers are just too big.

"But if that happened 10 times across a smaller group of people," said Freier, "they're going to talk about that. Because at the beginning of the day, they're going to have a huddle, at the end of the day, they're going to have a huddle. 'What did you hear? What are our customers telling us about?' 'Well, I had a customer, I can't believe they're calling in because they're going on a mission for two years and they're calling . . . ' 'Oh, I had that happen, too!' 'Me too!' And before you know it, because of that kind of an insight that a local team is having, you can then have a discussion about how we can solve that. In a national global call routing scheme, it's just almost impossible."

Notice that the data was always "in the system"! Missionaries had always called. Before TEX, though, the support team would have been blind to the pattern. But with the new model, when one person learned something important, everyone learned it.

The company had, in essence, built a better circulatory system for information. And that's the final step in our quest to stack up resources: the desire to accelerate our learning.

Whirlwind review: Chapter 10, Let People Drive

1. Letting people drive is the fifth way to Restack Resources. Autonomy works because it's motivating, it instills more accountability, it taps higher-order skills, and it reduces waste from micromanagement.
   a. *Richard Gibney allowed his patients to perform self-dialysis, and the results were strikingly positive. "The least utilized resource in medicine is the patient."*

2. In uncertain, anxiety-making situations, you may be tempted to grab for control. But that's the wrong instinct: You need to let people drive.
   a. *The archery coach Guy Krueger realized that he'd been micromanaging talented athletes who were more effective when THEY led the training.*
   b. *As we saw in chapter 7, excess management is waste—it squanders managerial time and caps employees' effectiveness.*

3. Autonomy is not an unbounded positive, though—either for the quality of the work or for the motivation of the employees. In a survey, people reported wanting guidance and support.

4. Spotify has a nice way of blending freedom and guidance. They try to support a high-autonomy, high-alignment culture.
   a. *"Leaders focus on what problems to solve, but let the teams figure out how to solve it."*

5. It's possible to shift to a high-autonomy, high-alignment culture with the right support systems and incentives.
   a. *At T-Mobile, the TEX model transformed customer service from a solo sport to a team sport. Each TEX team was given ownership over a set of customer relationships. The results benefited both the customers AND the employees.*

Recommendations (find live links at <u>danheath.com/reset-links</u>):

To see normal dialysis through the eyes of a first-time patient, read <u>Steve Winfree's account</u>. Also, to cry your eyeballs out, tune in for an unexpected twist in Winfree's life when his wife discovered later that she was an organ "match" and <u>surprised him with the news</u> that she would give him a kidney. You can read more about Dr. Gibney's self-care dialysis efforts and a similar initiative at a Dallas health care system in <u>this *Harvard Business Review* article</u>. For a deeper look at Gabriele Wulf's work on motivation and attention—mentioned in the context of the archery story—see her <u>2021 paper</u> (<u>open-access version</u>), coauthored with Rebecca Lewthwaite, which describes the OPTIMAL theory of performance. For more on Spotify's "alignment + autonomy" approach, watch <u>this video</u> created by Henrik Kniberg. For another bit of inspiration on letting people drive, listen to <u>this podcast episode</u> with James Daunt. Daunt is the independent bookseller who turned around Waterstones, the UK's largest book retailer. He did so, in large part, by empowering the staff to decide how they could best serve their communities. (I love his story but didn't have the space for it here.) If you enjoyed the T-Mobile TEX teams story, be sure to check out my original source, Matthew Dixon's "<u>Reinventing Customer Service</u>," published in 2018 in *Harvard Business Review*. It's admirably detailed and fun to read. (By the way I also loved Dixon's book *<u>The Effortless Experience</u>*, coauthored with Nick Toman and Rick DeLisi—essential reading for anyone looking to improve customer service.)

ACCELERATE LEARNING

>> You can Restack Resources on your Leverage Points by getting better, faster feedback to fuel improvements.

ACCELERATE LEARNING

1.

Moon Javaid, the chief strategy officer for the San Francisco 49ers, was the guy responsible for ensuring that 49ers fans had a good time at the team's games. For years, Javaid and his staff had relied on fan surveys to guide them.

Fans often complained, for example, about how long it took to get out of the parking lot after a game. One problem was that everybody took the shortest path to their own car. The result was chaos. No one could drive efficiently because there were people wandering everywhere.

So Javaid's team put up some ropes to channel the flow of people to different parts of the lot. Suddenly the parking lot looked more like an orderly Disney World queue than a Black Friday Walmart.

A few days after the end of the 2016 season, Javaid and his boss, Al Guido, the team president, were reviewing some possible changes based on fan feedback. *You know, we've only got 10 shots a year to get this right*, Guido said (referring to the number of 49ers home games, including the preseason). *So if we're just waiting for the next game to improve things, we've already missed 10% of the customer's experience.*

Guido challenged Javaid to make improvements in real time. Could they monitor fan feedback and act on it immediately?

Guido's "real-time data" prompt was a compelling idea for change, but Javaid had no idea how to accomplish it. No other NFL team had any kind of real-time feedback engine, much less the ability to act on that feedback instantly.

Javaid researched alternatives and found some survey apps that could compile data instantly. It was nifty technology, but he just couldn't imagine it working. Would 70,000 fans really pull out their phones during a game and do a survey? It seemed like a dead end.

Then, in an airport one day, he stumbled across a HappyOrNot terminal, a device designed to gather quick customer feedback. The terminals, often stationed just outside a TSA checkpoint or inside a bathroom, have four buttons: big smile, little smile, little frown, and big frown.*

Javaid had seen them before, but it suddenly clicked for him: *This could be my solution.* "I literally sat down for an hour, missed my flight on purpose, and just waited and watched to see if people would hit the button," he said. "I was actually surprised because I had never hit one of those buttons in my life but I saw a large number of people hit them. And I thought, okay, this could be interesting."

He imagined installing terminals outside concession stands. Inside bathrooms. Near the front gates. The stadium could be wired up—and for the first time, he could monitor the fan experience in real time.

---

*Coincidentally, this is also the exact sequence of emotions you experience every season as a Carolina Panthers fan . . .

Excited, Javaid called the HappyOrNot sales department, only to discover that they couldn't provide real-time data. The company typically sent out summary reports to clients on the day after data was collected. Which wouldn't work, of course. Next-day feedback was pointless for an event. *Yesterday, fans were super unhappy about Restroom 41. Just thought you should know.*

Javaid lobbied the HappyOrNot team to build out a real-time app for the 49ers. *We'll be your guinea pigs*, he told them, *and you can resell the tech to other customers*. The idea appealed to them, so they started designing it.

The 49ers quickly became a major account for HappyOrNot. The stadium had 600 points of sale and 50 restrooms, so in the past, no manager could keep tabs on everything. It was too much. "For an NFL game, you are going to have a lot of problems," said Javaid. "You're busing in about 3,500 temporary employees. You have 60,000 people coming in at one time. Buildings just aren't meant to be shocked like that. Toilets aren't meant to be flushed that way."

With 150 terminals installed at key locations, though, the fans' button pushes vastly expanded what the managers could monitor. During games, when a terminal logged a certain threshold of negative feedback—15 people complaining within a five-minute time-frame—it could automatically send alerts to the person in charge: *Get to Concession Stand B1*. Or *Get to Restroom 18*.

The app couldn't explain what was wrong. It just knew that people were unhappy. Initially the staffers were nervous about this ambiguity: What if they couldn't figure out what's wrong? But once they started using the system, they realized the problems were usually obvious: A toilet was clogged. The stand was out of hot-dog buns.

(One exception that proved a genuine mystery: During one game, the app flagged a concession stand that served alcohol. Lots of frowny-button pushes. The staff rushed there but couldn't detect a problem. After some fruitless investigation, they gave up, but the red alerts kept coming. Javaid insisted they go back until they figured out the problem, and eventually, they cracked it: A wine fridge was broken. Customers had been paying for warm white wine.)

By 2019, the 49ers were receiving 40,000 button pushes per game—40,000 new data points.* For the team, this avalanche of data proved difficult to analyze. Clogged toilets were easy to act on. But what else did all that data tell them? So Javaid's team invested in brain-friendly data visualizations that allowed them to see and understand the feedback in real time.

The visualizations also unearthed unexpected insights. With concessions, comparing numbers across games proved to be tricky. As an example, look at the two heat maps on the opposite page. The "x" marks show problem areas. The first map shows the fans' feedback in a game against the Cowboys. They are not happy—there are many trouble spots around the stadium.

The second image below shows the heat map a few weeks later, at a comparable point in the game against the Jaguars. Note there's only one trouble spot (at the top).

What would you guess went wrong in the Cowboys game (the top picture)? Supply outage? Staffing problem?

The explanation is that in the Cowboys game, the 49ers were losing. Badly. And that made everything seem worse: The bathrooms seemed dirtier. The beer didn't seem as cold.

---

*It's worth remarking on the fact that, when you make it INCREDIBLY EASY for people to give you useful feedback, you get more of it. Just smash one button on the way out of the bathroom! It's the polar opposite of those "How was your flight?" surveys that manage to sprawl across 16 soul-deadening screens. (Item 118: "On a scale of 1–7, how would you assess the flight attendants' posture?")

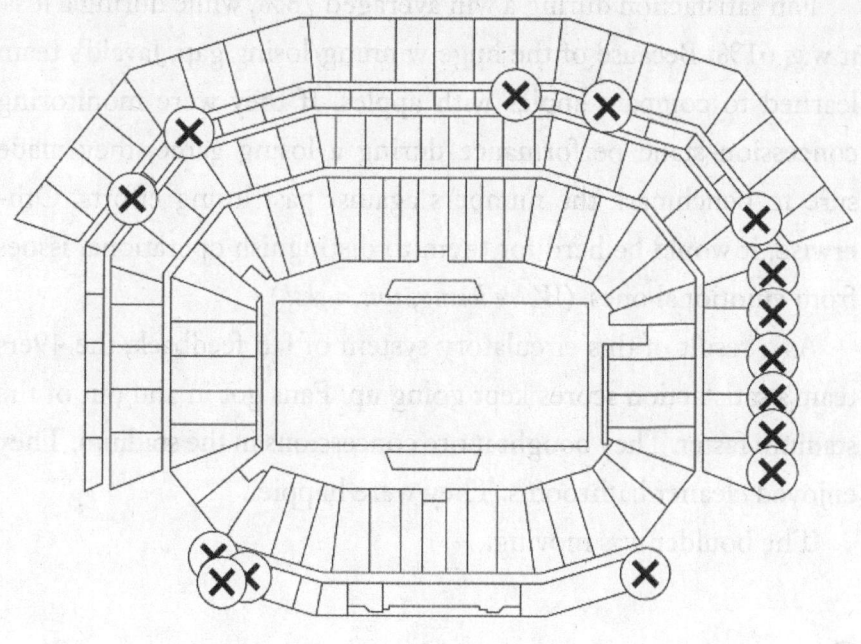

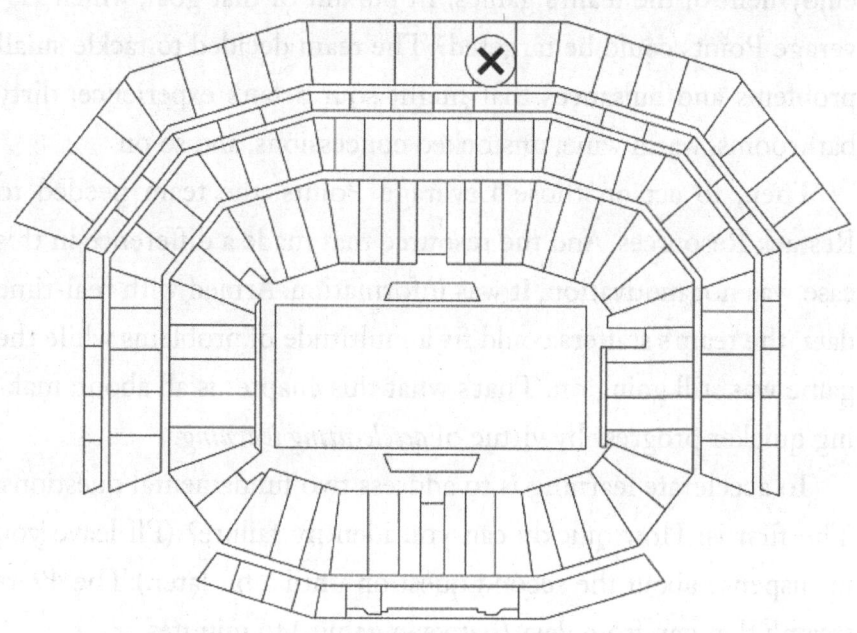

Fan satisfaction during a win averaged 78%, while during a loss, it was 61%. Because of the huge winning/losing gap, Javaid's team learned to compare apples with apples. If they were monitoring concession stand performance during a losing game, they made sure to benchmark the numbers against past losing efforts. Otherwise, it would be hard for them to distinguish operational issues from emotional ones. (*We're losing, this sucks!*)

As a result of this circulatory system of fan feedback, the 49ers team's satisfaction scores kept going up. Fans got in and out of the stadium faster. They bought more concessions in the stadium. They enjoyed cleaner bathrooms. They were happier.

The boulder was moving.

2.

Let's rewind the 49ers story. The leaders' goal was to boost fans' enjoyment of the team's games. In pursuit of that goal, which Leverage Points could be targeted? The team decided to tackle small problems and nuisances that might sour a fan's experience: dirty bathrooms, warm wine, unstocked concessions, and so on.

Then, to act on those Leverage Points, the team needed to Restack Resources. And the resource that made a difference in this case was not motivation, it was information. Armed with real-time data, the team's staffers could fix a multitude of problems while the game was still going on. That's what this chapter is all about: making quicker progress by virtue of *accelerating learning*.

To accelerate learning is to address two fundamental questions. The first is: How quickly can you identify failure? (I'll leave you in suspense about the second question until a bit later.) The 49ers shrunk that gap from days (between games) to minutes.

Notice that shrinking that lag time—the time needed to spot

failure—also involves a reduction in *waste*. If you think about it, the 49ers story is similar to the story of the Asheboro trash trucks from chapter 7. Before the HappyOrNot terminals were installed, the 49ers staffers had to patrol every bathroom, looking for the dirty ones, in the same way that the bulk trash trucks had to roll down every block, hunting for abandoned futons and fridges. But once the terminals were in place during the games, providing real-time feedback, those "routes" stopped operating by happenstance. Workers could go straight to where help was needed.

That's no accident. There's an organic link between these threads of "faster learning" and "reduced waste." They tend to twine together. Because learning involves recalibration: Do more of this, do less of that. That recalibration—learning to shift your efforts toward more valuable pursuits—is the same thing as reducing waste.

And it feels better, too—more motivating to the people involved. Moon Javaid said his team appreciated having the richer feedback. "I'm asking for things to get better and that tends to lead to asking people to do more work," he said. "But in this situation, it was actually heartwarming. I sat down with a manager after the first couple of weeks and he said, 'I love this because I have information that actually helps me to do my job.'"

The right information in the right moment is the ultimate navigational aid.

3.

Learning faster does not necessitate more technology or even more data. Sometimes it's just about seeking the right source of feedback. Remember Tom Chi? He's the innovation expert from chapter 1 who talked about how decisions are usually made by guess-a-thons. Years ago, he was approached by a multibillion-dollar global energy management company—let's call it Schmidt—that had a problem retaining executives. The company had been losing 70% of its top executives, on average, every three years.

Chi learned that Schmidt was organized in a decentralized fashion, with each country run by its own CEO, so that each region could be served more nimbly. Those CEOs were replaced every three to four years in order to maintain a constant stream of new ideas. And about two years into a CEO's term, they were expected to start succession planning for the person who would replace them in the next cycle.

These choices apparently gave Schmidt what it was looking for: lots of innovation and an antidote to complacency. But there was a costly side effect: Around the time when a particular CEO's successor was named, the executives who were passed over tended to depart.

How could Schmidt do a better job retaining those passed-over executives? The company's leaders had developed five proposals, which they shared with Chi to seek his feedback. Chi recalled, in a talk posted online, what happened next:

> CHI: What happened when you tried these [proposals] out?
> SCHMIDT: Oh, we didn't try these out yet.
> CHI: Hm, okay. That's a lot of work to not try. Did you just come up with these? Did you not have time to do it yet?
> ...
> SCHMIDT: Tom, I don't think you understand. This is really serious business. If we execute the wrong retention program, we might lose our top executives. [laughter in room]

The leaders had been agonizing over these proposals for months, but they hadn't really *done anything* yet. They were stuck in guess-a-thons. So Chi challenged them to tap a new source of feedback: their own executives. Facing a room full of Schmidt's top leaders, from different countries around the world, Chi staged a role-play.

He pulled over a table and invited the CEO of Brazil to sit there. *This is your desk*, Chi said.

Then Chi invited up another executive: *Pretend you're the COO of Brazil. You've been called in to meet with the CEO. You're excited because you think this might be the meeting where you get named the successor.*

Chi went back to the CEO of Brazil and said, "What's gonna happen is he's not gonna get the job, but you're gonna tell him about this amazing executive exchange program."

The "exchange program" was one of Schmidt's ideas for improving retention. The pitch was, basically, *Okay, you didn't get named the next CEO, but we really value your abilities, so we're going to swap you from Brazil to (say) Egypt, where you can join the team for a few years, solve some problems for them, and come back a hero!* The program was a well-intentioned consolation prize.

So the role-play begins. The COO enters the CEO's office. They shake hands and sit. The CEO cautiously and politely reveals that the COO will not be the successor, then pitches him on the executive exchange program. At first, the COO keeps a poker face. Then concern sprouts. His brow furrows.

A few minutes into the conversation, he pushes back from the table, saying, "That's enough. I've heard enough. Look, I've been a professional for over 20 years, I've been an executive for over 12 years. I understand sometimes you get the promotion, sometimes you don't. . . . But now what you're telling me is in order to continue to have a great career at Schmidt, I need to pull my kids out of school, convince my wife to move to a country where we don't even speak the language, work with a team I've never even met once, and abandon the team that, to your credit, is one of the best operational teams in all of Schmidt. You are crazy. I quit."

The exchange program had been Schmidt's favorite idea for a retention program! Then, within a few minutes of a role-play, they figured out the idea was a dog. How? By putting themselves in a situation where they could learn. "Discussing the idea" internally was not learning; it was one of Chi's guess-a-thons. But trying out the idea with people who were similar to the target audience—that's learning.

Imagine how long this charade could have continued absent Chi's involvement. It's possible that they would have debated it until eventually they talked themselves into rolling it out, investing millions in the program infrastructure, training the regions in how it worked, making plans for the relocations, and so forth. They could have spent *years* building out this terrible program before they realized it was terrible!

Accelerating learning allows you to limit—and even prevent—wasteful efforts.

4.

How quickly can you identify failure? The 49ers accelerated learning by deploying an army of HappyOrNot terminals. Schmidt accelerated learning by trying a role-play with the right audience. This same transformation—shrinking the time needed to surface failure—happened on a larger scale in the software industry over the last few decades. Until the 1990s, most software was developed using what's called the "waterfall" approach. It's called "waterfall" in tribute to the linear, cascading flow of the project stages:

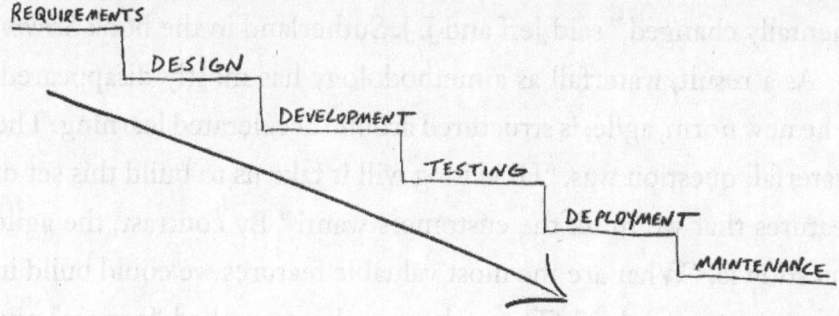

There are countless reasons why the waterfall approach didn't work: People are lousy at estimating how long it will take to do something (the so-called "planning fallacy"). As a result, the projects were usually egregiously behind the schedule. (Old heads will remember that major OS releases, such as Windows, frequently seemed to take *years* longer than expected.)*

Waterfall also encouraged long periods of slack until the team got into crisis mode close to the deadline—akin to a college student who waits until the night before to write the 10-page term paper.

But the fundamental problem with waterfall was that *many teams did not get substantive feedback from actual customers until late in the development cycle*. Which might be years! That was a fatal flaw. Because sometimes you got to the end of the cycle—ready to ship software—only to get a nasty surprise.

"I see this happen all the time: a company will spend years on a project that seemed like a good idea when the workers started on

---

*Windows 95, for instance, was delayed multiple times, but when it finally launched, it at least came with a proper release: Jay Leno hosted the launch party. Jennifer Aniston and Matthew Perry from *Friends* did a promo video. The Rolling Stones, trailblazing a new low for rock sellouts, licensed "Start Me Up."

it, but by the time they cross the finish line, the market has fundamentally changed," said Jeff and J. J. Sutherland in the book *Scrum*.

As a result, waterfall as a methodology has mostly disappeared. The new norm, agile, is structured around accelerated learning. The waterfall question was, "How long will it take us to build this set of features that we think the customers want?" By contrast, the agile question is, "What are the most valuable features we could build in the next two weeks?" (These short cycles are called "sprints" and their length varies, but they are denominated in weeks, not years.)

You build a little, test it, get feedback, build a little more, and so on. Because it's iterative, there's little chance of a product unveiling where the customer says, *No, this is garbage, this is not what I need at all*. Because you've been in touch with them all along. The customer's voice is connected to your operations via a reliable feedback loop.

Let's get back to the first question of accelerating learning: How quickly can you identify failure? With waterfall, it might take years. With agile, it would take weeks or, at worst, a few months.

But agile is not just a "failure detection" methodology. It's also about unlocking improvements. And that brings us to the second key question of accelerating learning: How quickly can you spot potential successes? Because when you understand your customers better, and when you observe how they use your products, you can also spot *opportunities*.

Learning is not just about avoiding or minimizing failure, it's about maximizing success. To see how these two goals can intersect, consider Eric Nuzum's work at National Public Radio (NPR). Nuzum took inspiration from agile principles when, in 2011, he was put in charge of programming. He was charged with developing a slate of promising new shows.

The time was ripe for innovation: NPR had a stable of popular programs, such as the Saturday morning favorite *Car Talk*, but there was a weak pipeline of up-and-coming shows that might become hits. NPR's programming was in danger of aging out.

Traditionally, developing shows had been a labor-intensive, costly, and slow proposition. The network would hatch a new show idea, incubate it slowly and secretly, pour millions of dollars into its development, find a star to be the host, then unveil it a year or two later to great fanfare. And then they would wait even more months and years to see whether the show was a hit or a flop. (Sound familiar? That's essentially the waterfall model.)

So, challenged with cultivating a crop of new shows, Nuzum requested millions of dollars to fund development.

He got zero.

"So I can't do it the old way," he said. "I started asking myself questions about how I can short-circuit parts of this process."

Nuzum cobbled together a new development process, a quick and dirty one. Now, when someone came up with a promising idea for a show, they'd start working on a "paper pilot." Instead of investing enormous resources in producing "pilots"—inaugural episodes of a new show—Nuzum's idea was: Why don't we do some futzing around on paper first, before we start recording anything?

The paper pilot asked a lot of basic questions: What would happen in the first few episodes of this show? What kinds of guests would we invite, and where would we find them? What recurring features would we have on the show?

The paper pilot provided an immediate payoff: It helped to detect underbaked ideas. "Many times people have ideas for podcasts or radio shows that sound great," said Nuzum. "And then once you actually say, 'Okay, let's sketch out what three episodes of this would look like,' you realize it's not really a series. It's an episode. It's one hour of good material, really."

The paper pilot also allowed the team to practice collaborating. Sometimes the results could be surprising. At one point, the team had gotten excited about a show centered on food. For the host role, they had recruited an editor of a prestigious food magazine. She seemed perfect.

They started drafting the paper pilot, working alongside the editor, only to discover that she "was just kind of a diva and was not fun to work with and was very immediately dismissive of ideas," said Nuzum. The staff "was actively trying to avoid her."

The feedback from the paper pilot, then, allowed them to turn a long, drawn-out debacle into a quick and disposable trial. (*How quickly can you identify failure?*)

He captured the spirit of his new approach with an analogy: "The historical way [we developed shows] was to take a pack of tomato seeds and spread them out on the table. And everyone would argue about which seed was going to be the one that germinated and had the most fruit."

Together they would crown the Most Promising Seed. Then, they would pour massive resources into it and "everyone would sit there and wring their hands to see if it sprouted and if it bore fruit and how much fruit," he said.

The flaw with this process is clear: "A gardener will tell you to plant a bunch of different seeds because half of them aren't even going to germinate," he said. "And the ones that do germinate, some are going to be all twisted and messed up and never really develop to the right size, and only a small number of them will develop fruit. . . . To develop tomatoes—get really great tomatoes—you have to start with a bunch of different seeds."

One word of caution here: Nuzum's analogy is not an argument for self-disempowerment: *I can't possibly know anything about what will succeed, so I might as well toss a bunch of random seeds into the ground and see what happens.* That's not what he's saying. Nuzum and his team knew an enormous amount about what made shows succeed! They could probably dismiss 90% of their show ideas out of hand, just based on their accumulated experience.

The point is that for the remaining 10%, there was no reason to "guess" about which one would fare best. Just plant the seeds. To get back to Nuzum's analogy, you want to start with the best seeds from the best growers, and use the best soil and fertilizer, and then let nature take its course.

Testing is a replacement for guessing, not a replacement for judgment.

So Nuzum started with multiple seeds. Some of those initial ideas made it to the paper pilot stage. Some of the paper pilots were promising enough that a real pilot was taped. Some of those pilots were strong enough that a full season was funded. And some of those shows became hits.

Megahits, in fact. Some of those tomato seeds turned into *TED Radio Hour*, *Ask Me Another*, *Hidden Brain*, and *Invisibilia*. Some of the biggest radio and podcasting successes of the past 20 years.

5.

How quickly can you identify failure? How quickly can you spot potential successes?

Nuzum's agile-inspired approach answered *both* questions: It revealed failures more quickly, as with the cooking show. And it also managed to incubate good ideas more quickly, by giving more "seeds" the opportunity to thrive without breaking the budget.

The 49ers, too, actually learned to use the incoming data to spot opportunities as well as failures. In studying the visualizations of the concession stands, Moon Javaid looked for anomalies: Maybe there would be one red dot (an underperforming stand) right in between two green dots (thriving stands). Given that data, he'd know that the problem with the red dot wasn't the location, it was the concept.

"At the end of every season, we would replace all those red dots with new concepts—for example, we could try a chicken tenders concept that might resonate with fans," he said.

And this tinkering with red dots worked: When they swapped out a stand, the average improvement was about 15%.

We've come full circle, then, to the beginning of the book. Because those red dots, for Javaid, were basically an invitation to find a new Leverage Point. A new idea for change that would improve the fan's experience.

The book's framework—Finding Leverage Points and Restacking Resources—is usually iterative.* You identify a priority and then you push on it. If it doesn't go the way you hoped, you learn from the experience. Maybe there's a better direction to push. (The 49ers used data to learn how to deploy their staffers' time more effectively.) Or maybe you identify a better priority. (At NPR, planting multiple seeds allowed them to invest in more promising shows.)

Quick adaptation is the ultimate force multiplier. If we aspire to get unstuck and make progress on what matters, we must accelerate our learning.

---

*Usually, but not always. And I think this is an important nuance. Personally, I do not believe that all change needs to be iterative, in the spirit of methodologies such as "continuous improvement." Sometimes it's enough simply to step from one plateau to a better one: You lose 10 pounds and then you hold at the new weight. Or, to revisit the ExxonMobil Technical Data Center story, you and your team do a "burst" to whittle down some towering piles of unarchived files. Sometimes positive change is a one-off: You do it and it's done. The system is fixed. That's still a reset! And those changes are well worth fighting for!

Whirlwind review: Chapter 11, Accelerate Learning

1. The sixth and final way to Restack Resources on your Leverage Points is to accelerate your learning. The faster you can learn, the faster you can go.

2. The first question of accelerating learning is: How quickly can you identify failure?
   a. *When the 49ers deployed the HappyOrNot terminals around the stadium, the real-time data helped them send staffers directly to the trouble spots, thus preventing more customer dissatisfaction. Before using the terminals, it would have taken a week—not minutes—to adapt.*

3. Useful feedback helps you align resources with goals. That tight calibration cuts waste, which is one of the key themes of Restacking.
   a. *The 49ers story is similar to the Asheboro trucks tale in chapter 7 on recycling waste: The right information lets workers go directly to where their help was most needed.*

4. Learning faster doesn't necessarily demand more data or technology. Sometimes it hinges on seeking out the people best equipped to give feedback.
   a. *At Schmidt, leaders had dreamed up an "exchange program" as a consolation prize for executives who were not named regional CEOs. But they learned quickly that the program was a dog when Tom Chi had the sense to test it out with a group of senior executives.*

5. The second question of accelerating learning is: How quickly can you spot potential successes?
   a. *Notice that the innovation of agile development answered both questions: It helped teams spot failure quicker (by speeding up the development cycles), but it also helped them spot successes by bringing them closer to the customer's voice.*
   b. *At NPR, Eric Nuzum stopped trying to "pick the best tomato seed." Instead, he created a method for testing multiple show concepts at once, more akin to planting multiple seeds and seeing which ones grew. This allowed more shows a chance to thrive.*

6. The right information in the right moment is the ultimate navigational aid. If we want to make progress on what matters, we must accelerate our learning.

Recommendations (find live links at <u>danheath.com/reset-links</u>):

Here's my second plug for the <u>talk by Tom Chi</u> that I recommended in chapter 1. For those looking to understand both how to learn faster and why it's important, there's no better introduction. I'd also be remiss not to plug the excellent <u>Scrum</u> here. The book provides an overview of the agile approach that has replaced waterfall and supercharged teams in the tech industry and beyond, from military operations to hospital administration to a high school science class. <u>Practice Perfect</u> by Doug Lemov, Erica Woolway, and Katie Yezzi is a great tool for shrinking the learning loop in your organization—it's especially relevant for teaching and coaching. (I liked it so much I wrote a foreword for it.) If you're a creative type, and especially if you have an interest in audio storytelling in particular, don't miss Eric Nuzum's book <u>Make Noise</u>, which further explores the benefits and clarity that come with getting your great ideas (and the not-so-great ones) down on paper. For more on the HappyOrNot terminals used by the San Francisco 49ers, check out David Owen's New Yorker <u>story</u> "Customer Satisfaction at the Push of a Button," which traces their fascinating history. (The first installation was in a small grocery store in western Finland.)

Conclusion

1.

In 2018, Wania Regina Mollo Baia—a nurse and director at a major hospital in São Paulo, Brazil—needed a final project for her training program. She had been part of a cohort, led by Jessica Perlo at the IHI, that was dedicated to instilling "Joy at Work." The cohort had been studying the question: *How do you create a joyful, engaged workforce?*

In health care, that could be a difficult mission. In many places around the world, the sector was characterized by staff burnout, high turnover, and low morale. Similar problems affected Baia's employer, Hospital Sírio-Libanês, one of Brazil's most respected health care institutions.

Put yourself in Baia's shoes: You want to lead a project that will actually lift your colleagues' engagement and happiness at work. That's an ambitious goal! That's a boulder. How do you move it?

Well, you know the answer by now: You Find a Leverage Point and you Restack Resources on it. Baia's approach provides a nice opportunity to review the full scope of what we've explored in the book—first, let's dive into the story (without constant authorial interruptions) and then we'll circle back and map her efforts to the book's framework.

In her training cohort, Baia had been introduced to the IHI's model of "Joy at Work," which included nine independent factors, ranging from "wellness & resilience" to "camaraderie & teamwork" to "recognition & rewards." Of these nine factors, there was one in particular that popped out for Baia: "participative management," meaning that workers are given a voice in their work and allowed the opportunity to "co-produce joy."

That factor was a particular pain point for Hospital Sírio-Libanês. In a recent survey of critical care staffers, only 40% had agreed with the statement: "I participate in local decisions that affect my work." Baia thought if she could move that number, it would make a powerful difference.

So she hatched an idea for a project—*What matters to you?*—and pitched it to her colleagues, from administrators to nurses to physical therapists. "I felt it was important for me to be 100% honest with them so whenever they would ask me: 'Is this going to work?' I would say: 'I have no idea if this is going to work,'" said Baia. "We held hands and jumped right in."

Under her plan, staffers were asked to consider: What makes a good day? What makes you proud to work here? When we are at our best, what does that look like? They were asked to write their answers on sticky notes and post them on a public bulletin board.*

At the same time, they were asked: *What are the impediments to what matters?* That is, what are the organizational obstacles to

---

*It occurs to me that this is the FOURTH appearance of sticky notes in the book: (1) the batching exercise in the hospital receiving area; (2) "sticky-note appreciations"; (3) genius swap; and (4) this work in Brazil. I think/hope this is coincidence and that successful change does not, in fact, depend on scraps of paper with light adhesive. That said, this could be a business opportunity: If you work at 3M, contact me about securing naming rights for the next edition of the book.

experiencing more of a sense of purpose? More sticky notes were added, reflecting those blockers. Soon the board overflowed with gripes, complaints, and barriers. (Samples: *There's no team spirit among colleagues—it's everyone for themselves; The schedule on the weekend is rough; The coffee machine never works on the night shift.*)

"When I got to the board and saw 300 Post-Its, for instance, I thought to myself: 'What the heck? Where was I that I didn't see all these demands before?'" said Nilda Rosa de Oliveira Prado, a colleague of Baia's.

Over a few weeks, the response to both prompts—What matters to you? And what blocks the things that matter?—proliferated until the whole board was crammed:

Baia and Prado knew they couldn't stop there. Otherwise the gripes would just form a "wailing wall," as Prado said, and that wasn't the spirit of the exercise.

So they grouped the impediments into themes, prioritizing the themes that were cited most often. The biggest gripe, by far, was the way workers were scheduled. That was a thorny issue. But not all of the complaints were so big and systemic. The seventh most popular theme covered frustrations about . . . the coffee machine.

After the top frustrations were identified, the staffers organized themselves into teams (all voluntary), by theme, to offer recommendations to mitigate or eliminate the impediments. Baia and her colleagues encouraged them to think in terms of quick wins: *What's something we can do right away in our area to make progress on this? Like, within 24 hours?*

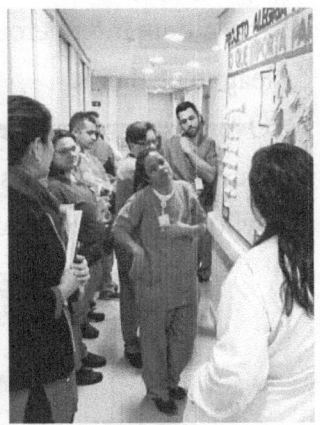

These were mostly "stone in the shoe" issues—small issues that, if resolved, would deliver a lot of relief. The key word being "resolved." Baia had done careful advance work to make sure that the hospital's senior leaders were ready to say "yes" to all reasonable requests. No delays, no bureaucracy, no instinctive resistance. *If we're going to invite people to identify problems and do the actual work of resolving them, then we've got to get out of their way and let them drive.*

Some of the issues were addressed quickly. The coffee machine got replaced. A "Recognition Tree" was added to provide a place to honor staffers. By popular demand, a closet was dedicated to each shift (morning, afternoon, and night) to provide space for clothes to change into—for instance, so they could watch the World Cup games in proper team attire.

Not all of the issues were so easy. Scheduling, in particular, was a bear. The existing model was baked deep into the systems of the hospital. Many staffers worked six 6-hour days, with a day off on the seventh day. A substantial contingent of them lobbied for three 12-hour shifts, scheduled every other day to allow for rest.

The administrators were skeptical. In the past, the idea would have simply been vetoed. This time, though, it was tested. A group of nurses tried the three 12-hour shifts and it proved popular not only with the nurses but also, unexpectedly, with their patients. The patients liked getting to spend more time with the same nurse—it provided more continuity. They didn't have to repeat all their issues to a new staffer every 6 hours.

On the strength of the positive outcomes from the testing, the new 12-hour shift schedule—which had initially seemed radical— became the new norm. The other tests conducted by the working groups were similarly successful: More than 93% of the ideas that they tested were ultimately implemented.

As Baia's project continued, its progress was carefully monitored. The "trackability" of participative management had been one of the things that attracted her to the concept.

One of the working groups concocted a simple guerrilla idea for making progress visible. Medical and support staffers, after con- cluding a shift, were asked to choose either an orange or a white Ping-Pong ball. A white ball signified, *This was a collaborative and participatory shift*. An orange ball signified the opposite. The person would drop the ball they'd chosen into a transparent community bin (that's the empty bin on the right below):

As a result, you could look at the community bin, stuffed with balls, and quickly get a feel for how the day had gone. In the beginning of the effort, orange balls outnumbered white ones, but as the days rolled on, white came to dominate:

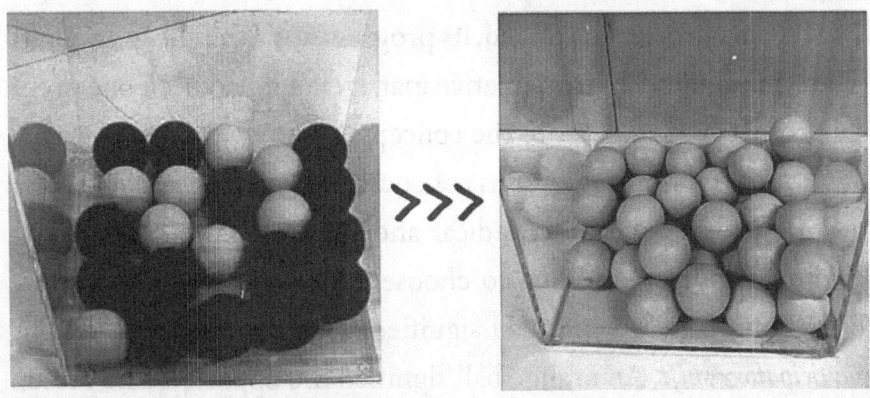

Everybody could see: *This is working*.

Baia and her colleagues used the rigor of continuous improvement to monitor the change. They tracked the percentage of employees who agreed with this statement: "I participate in local decisions that affect my work."

The results were striking: The number of employees who agreed with that statement vaulted up from 40% to 69% within six months of the start of the project. And the number *stayed high*. Two years after the pilot project, it had reached 72%.

As Baia had predicted, this success—making employees feel heard and listened to—had ripple effects. In employee surveys, numbers were up over 10 percentage points on feelings of respect, camaraderie, pride, and more. Retention improved. Even patient outcomes improved: The number of adverse events declined substantially.

This stunning success created its own momentum with Hospital Sírio-Libanês. Other groups within the hospital rushed to embrace the same game plan. By 2021, it had been rolled out across the hospital. Then leaders from other hospitals came calling, wanting to import the idea to their own organizations. Baia organized a cohort of hospitals across Brazil to learn from her successful efforts to create "Joy at Work."

"I have always wanted to see all health care professionals become more of the protagonists in the system, as opposed to them being invisible," said Baia.

When your employees are consulted, they will contribute. When they are empowered, they will act. When they are trusted, they will lead.

2.

Now let's zoom out for a minute. I absolutely love this story for two reasons: First, it's immediately practical. There is nothing hospital- or Brazil-specific about this example. You can adopt a similar methodology with your own team. Just steal this game plan!

Second, the story provides a great chance to review the lessons of the book. I'll point to some different aspects of the story and remind you what those moments are illustrating.

Let's start with the way Baia targeted the issue of "participative management." That's a classic example of selecting a Leverage Point. You can't do everything, but you can do something. Make it a well-chosen something.

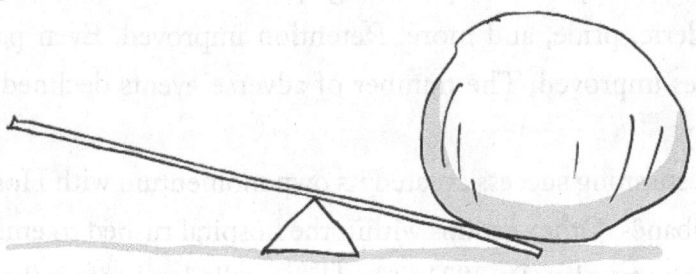

How did she select this particular Leverage Point? Partly it was a story of finding the *bright spots*—the IHI's model of Joy at Work came from distilling the best work of different health systems. (This is reminiscent of the Million Cat Challenge and how Kate Hurley discovered the bright spot of "return to field" at the Jacksonville shelter.)

The "participative management" Leverage Point was attentive to the *constraints* of the hospital, since the lack of agency was holding employees back. And it reflected Baia's belief that participative management was a "hidden lever" that could influence many others. (*Map the system.*)

Having identified "participative management" as a Leverage Point, how did Baia begin to Restack Resources?

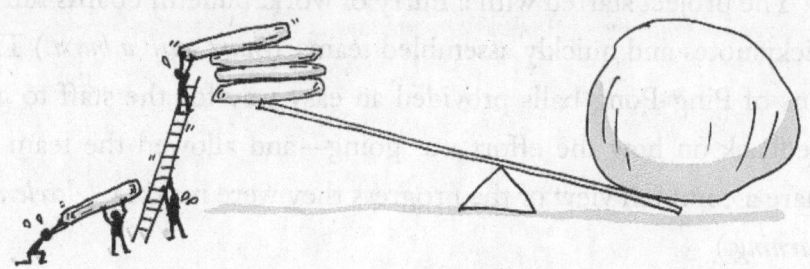

Well, remember: She asked the staffers, "What matters to you?" The entire project was architected to resolve exactly the things that employees said they cared about. (That's *tapping motivation*, of course.) Remember this Venn diagram—this was Baia's strategy:

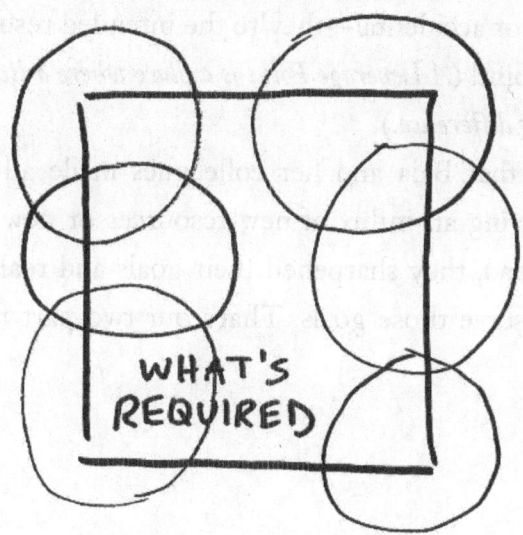

After identifying the staff's top frustrations—the factors that *interfered* with the things that mattered most to them—Baia let them volunteer to tackle those issues personally. They were put in charge: The change channeled their ideas and their leadership, and the hospital executives tried to say "yes" as much as possible. (*Let people drive.*)

The project started with a flurry of work: bulletin boards full of sticky notes and quickly assembled teams. (*Start with a burst.*) The bins of Ping-Pong balls provided an easy way for the staff to get feedback on how the effort was going—and allowed the team to share a common view of the progress they were making. (*Accelerate learning.*)

That progress created its own momentum: It was the proof that change was happening, that people were being listened to, which was motivating. (That's the progress principle.)

The core Leverage Point—improving employee sentiment on the statement "I participate in local decisions that affect my work"—had ripple effects, just as Baia had predicted. Feelings of respect and pride went up. Retention improved. These ripple effects are not lucky or accidental—they're the intended result of Finding a Leverage Point! (*A Leverage Point is a place where a little investment can make a big difference.*)

And note that Baia and her colleagues made all this happen without receiving an influx of new resources or new staff or new benefits. Instead, they sharpened their goals and reallocated their resources to serve those goals. That's our two-part framework in action.

3.

Baia and her colleagues reset the culture at Hospital Sírio-Libanês. Probably all of us can take inspiration from a success like that, but somehow, when it comes to changing our own organizations, we think, "Well, that could never happen here." We're worn down by past failed efforts. Or demoralized by the difficulty of playing politics or overcoming bureaucracy.

Sometimes we adopt a defeatist attitude: *It will take an emergency before anything changes around here.* And to be fair, that's partly right. People do change quickly in response to emergencies. Look at humanity's response to COVID: health systems were reimagined, schools went remote, businesses overhauled supply chains, vaccines were developed, massive government programs were hatched and rolled out . . . all in a matter of months. Months!

For a less extreme example: In June 2023, a tanker truck carrying gasoline exploded beneath an I-95 overpass in Philadelphia, melting the metal support beams and causing the bridge to collapse onto the highway, rendering the highway impassable. Experts predicted it would take months before the road could be restored, and as a result, the economic consequences would be dire, since I-95 is a critical transportation artery.

Nope. Twelve days later, traffic was flowing. The ingenious improvised solution involved building a temporary column that could support the overpass, allowing traffic to flow even as the permanent reconstruction was underway. The column was filled with 8,000 cubic yards (36,000 wheelbarrowsful) of foamed glass aggregate, made partly from recycled beer bottles. When the job was complete, all the Philadelphia sports team mascots rode together in a fire truck over the newly opened overpass. The governor threw a party for the construction workers.

So, yes, when people are forced to change, their capacity for change is vast. But let's not forget there's another option: People can *choose* to change.

This book was full of situations where people chose to change. No emergency forced their hand.

Quick progress happened at the radiology clinic described in chapter 5. A team was assembled with a charter to make things run better, and they made it happen: The receptionist started giving out oral contrast, the technologists stopped chaperoning the patients, and patient flow was improved dramatically. There was no emergency. Change was a choice. And they vaulted forward in five days.

Quick progress happened with Guy Krueger, the archery coach (chapter 10). Frustrated with his poor relationships with athletes, he went looking for answers and embraced a new coaching philosophy that *let athletes drive*. There was no emergency. Change was a choice. And his career thrived as a result.

Quick progress happened at Chick-fil-A (chapter 4). The team members pursued bottleneck after bottleneck, speeding up the drive-thru and breaking their own records for flow. There was no crisis. Change was a choice. And month after month, they kept getting better.

Quick progress happened throughout this book: The team in the hospital receiving area started delivering packages within a day. The Technical Data Center group at ExxonMobil triumphed over its mountain of unarchived files. The client partners at Gartner reversed the company's sliding customer retention numbers.

49ers games got better. Church services got shorter. Millions of cats were saved. A final father-and-son game of Ping-Pong was played. There was no emergency that compelled action in any of these situations. They were choices.

When we manage to budge the boulder, it serves us on two distinct levels: We (by definition) make progress toward our goals, which is remarkable enough. But, beyond that, as we witness ourselves moving, we simultaneously reassure ourselves that we're *capable* of moving.

We're not stuck. Not wheel-spinning. Not bogged down. Not stymied. Not paralyzed. Not depressed. Not defeated.

We're rolling forward.

And what could feel better than making progress toward something that matters?

Next Steps

You've finished *Reset*. Here's where to go next for FREE resources:

http://www.danheath.com/reset

When you sign up for the Heath Brothers newsletter, you'll get access to free materials like these: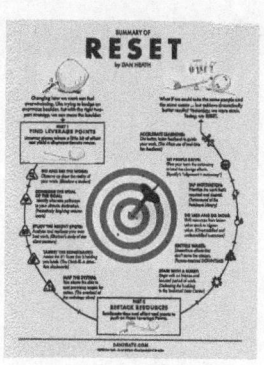

Reset **Summary.** You can download a bigger, prettier color version of the 1-page summary of this book. (The smaller, monochrome version is on the next page, if you want to glance at it.) Perfect for tacking up next to your desk.

 **Reset: Where to Start.** Ready to move a boulder in your organization but not quite sure where to start? In this video, I present some quick tips on taking your first few steps.

Book Club Guide. If you're reading *Reset* as part of a book club, this guide offers suggested questions and topics to guide your discussion.

 **Bonus: From the Cutting Room Floor.** In every book, there are ideas and stories that get cut. Read one of Dan's favorite passages that didn't quite fit. It's about "closing the loop."

SUMMARY OF

R E S E T

by DAN HEATH

Changing how we work can feel overwhelming. Like trying to budge an enormous boulder. But with the right two-part strategy, we can move the boulder.

What if we could take the same people and the same assets ... but achieve dramatically better results? Yesterday, we were stuck. Today, we RESET.

PART 1
FIND LEVERAGE POINTS
Uncover places where a little bit of effort can yield a disproportionate return.

ACCELERATE LEARNING:
Get better, faster feedback to guide your work. (The 49ers use of real-time fan feedback)

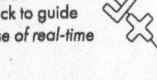

GO AND SEE THE WORK:
Observe up close the reality of your work. (Shadow a student)

LET PEOPLE DRIVE:
Give your team the autonomy to lead the change efforts. (Spotify's "alignment + autonomy")

CONSIDER THE GOAL OF THE GOAL:
Identify alternate pathways to your ultimate destination. (Proactively forgiving veteran loans)

TAP MOTIVATION:
Prioritize the work that's required and desired. (Turnaround of the Pottsboro Library)

STUDY THE BRIGHT SPOTS:
Analyze and replicate your own best work. (Gartner's study of star client partners)

DO LESS AND DO MORE:
Shift resources from lower-value work to higher-value. (Overcoddled and undercoddled customers)

TARGET THE CONSTRAINT:
Assess the #1 force that is holding you back. (The Chick-fil-A drive-thru cluckworks)

RECYCLE WASTE:
Discontinue efforts that don't serve the mission. (Toyota-inspired DOWNTIME)

MAP THE SYSTEM:
Rise above the silos to spot promising targets for action. (The overhaul of the radiology clinic)

START WITH A BURST:
Begin with an intense and focused period of work. (Defeating the backlog in the Technical Data Center)

PART 2
RESTACK RESOURCES
Reallocate time and effort and assets to push on those Leverage Points.

Acknowledgments

First and foremost, thank you to the readers who provided feedback on early drafts of this book. (You, reading this book, owe them a debt of gratitude, too—whatever you thought of this book, it would have been a lot worse without their help.) Early readers, I am so thankful that you took the time to offer suggestions, criticisms, questions, and recommendations.

This book would not exist without the contributions of my core research team: Evan Nesterak, Heather Graci, and Andrew Chaikivsky. They stuck with me across many iterations (and sooo many titles!) and enriched the manuscript in too many ways to cite. A heartfelt thank-you to the three of you for your creativity and your conscientiousness.

When you're in the middle of a book project and you're not sure what's working, good feedback is the most precious commodity imaginable. I want to single out Ken Davis, Nick Carnes, Jake Knapp, and Chip Heath for their repeated wise counsel. (And a double thank-you to Jake for the amazing illustrations—and the original idea to use them at all!)

Thanks to Peter Griffin for his editing prowess—and to Chris Grace and Dave Vance for adding some extra flair. And thanks to Christy Darnell for presiding over many rounds of reader feedback.

I feel so lucky to have worked with the same core team for so many years: Christy Fletcher and Sarah Fuentes and the team at

United Talent. And this was my fourth book with the master editor and bridge shark Ben Loehnen. (I am going to start hitting more fast-food drive-thrus in hopes of jostling loose the topic for a fifth collaboration ...) Thank you to everyone at Avid Reader Press who helped bring the book to life.

And most important, I am boundlessly grateful to my family: Amanda, Josephine, and Julia. I couldn't do any of this without you.

Notes

INTRODUCTION

ix **Northwestern Memorial Hospital receiving area:** This story is drawn from a case study, a series of interviews, and a visit to the receiving area in April 2022. John Nicholas, Hussam Bachour, and Paul Suett authored a case study and teaching note that detail the receiving area turnaround: Nicholas, J., Bachour, H., & Suett, P. (2019). "Northwestern Memorial Hospital: Smoothing Material Flow through the Receiving Area." Ivey Publishing. Interviews with Paul Suett over the course of 2022–2024, Frank Marasso in April 2024, and Charles Shipley in April 2024.

xi **Paul Batalden:** Batalden's "Every system is perfectly designed . . ." quote comes from this 2014 video about creating sustainably improving health care: https://www.youtube.com/watch?v=doQOKmrptDU. Batalden's quote also appears in Dan's book *Upstream*—see for example the example of how the Chicago Public School district unwittingly created a system with high dropout rates (and then, more inspiringly, turned it around).

xxi **The progress principle:** The research on the progress principle is drawn from Teresa Amabile and Steven Kramer's book: Amabile, T., & Kramer, S. (2011). *The Progress Principle: Using Small Wins to Ignite Joy, Engagement, and Creativity at Work.* Brighton, MA: Harvard Business Review Press; and their article "The Power of Small Wins," *Harvard Business Review*, May 2011, https://hbr.org/2011/05/the-power-of-small-wins.

CHAPTER 1 (GO AND SEE THE WORK)

5 **Shadow a student:** The shadow a student story is drawn from an interview with Karen Ritter in January 2024, and this report by *PBS*

NewsHour in 2016: https://www.pbs.org/newshour/show/one-assistant
-principal-learned-shadowing-student-day. The "Shadow a Student
Challenge" is also described on the Stanford d.school website: https://
dschool.stanford.edu/shadow-a-student-k12.

7   **Nelson Repenning:** Nelson Repenning's advice to "go and see the
work" and related stories come from an interview in October 2023
and articles published by MIT and the *MIT Sloan Management Review*.
Dylan Walsh describes Repenning's advice in "Four steps to improve
workplace safety and operations," MIT Sloan School of Management,
February 10, 2027, https://mitsloan.mit.edu/ideas-made-to-matter
/four-steps-to-improve-workplace-safety-and-operations. The quote
"When you go see the work, if you aren't embarrassed by what you
find, you probably aren't looking closely enough," comes from an article by Nelson Repenning, Don Kieffer, and Todd Astor, "The Most
Underrated Skill in Management," *MIT Sloan Management Review*,
March 13, 2017, https://sloanreview.mit.edu/article/the-most-under
rated-skill-in-management/. The corrugating machine story comes
from an article by Nelson Repenning, Don Kieffer, and Michael Morales, "Saving Money Through Structured Problem Solving," *MIT
Sloan Management Review*, March 21, 2017, https://sloanreview.mit
.edu/article/saving-money-through-structured-problem-solving/.
Repenning discusses the challenges of knowledge work in this 2021
talk for MIT Sloan Executive Education: https://www.youtube.com
/watch?v=pJwU-MZckTk.

11 **Tom Chi:** The insights and stories from Tom Chi come from an interview in April 2024 and two talks: "Getting Effective Session Outcomes"
at Google Design in 2018, https://www.youtube.com/watch?v=z_elg
zL9sns, and "Knowing is the enemy of learning" at TEDxSemesterat
Sea in 2014, https://www.youtube.com/watch?v=_WtsMrkfG1w.

13 **Illusion of explanatory depth:** The phenomenon is discussed in
Rozenblit, L., & Keil, F. (2002). "The misunderstood limits of folk
science: An illusion of explanatory depth." *Cognitive Science* 26(5),
521–62. The bicycle example comes from Lawson, R. (2006). "The science of cycology: Failures to understand how everyday objects work."
Memory and Cognition 34(8), 1667–75. (The bike drawings are used
with permission from the author.) Alex Nickel asks his peers about
how a toilet works in this 2017 video: https://www.youtube.com
/watch?v=9CodKUa4F2o.

15 **Business turnarounds:** The section on business turnarounds draws from an interview with Jeff Vogelsang in January 2023 and conversation on Dan's podcast, *What It's Like to Be . . .* : https://www.whatits liketobe.com/2246914/14607928-a-turnaround-consultant. Additional information on turnarounds: https://turnaround.org/business -assistance. The quote from Paul Fioravanti comes from "Turnaround expert, seeing the big picture" on *The Turnaround* (podcast) in 2020: https://open.spotify.com/episode/1jWZbLhO7eNHJyIkE4IMbK.

CHAPTER 2 (CONSIDER THE GOAL OF THE GOAL)

23 **Truck-buying story:** The survey shakedown story comes from an interview with Ryan Davidsen in September 2022, as well as documents and communications shared by Davidsen.

27 **Rory Sutherland:** Sutherland describes the Eurostar thought experiment in two talks, a 2009 TED Talk, "Life lessons from an ad man," https://www.ted.com/talks/rory_sutherland_life_lessons_from_an_ad _man, and a 2011 TEDx talk, "Perspective is everything," https://www .ted.com/talks/rory_sutherland_perspective_is_everything. Information on the Eurostar pricing was drawn from Jeremy Lovell's article "Eurostar makes high-speed London to Paris trip," Reuters, November 15, 2007, https://www.reuters.com/article/uk-britain-eurostar/eurostar -makes-high-speed-london-to-paris-trip-idUKL1484614120071114/, and Eric Pfanner's article, "Eurostar finally getting up to speed in Britain," *New York Times*, October 11, 2007, https://www.nytimes.com /2007/10/11/world/europe/11iht-eurostar.5.7858614.html.

28 **Marisa Lavars:** Lavars shared her New Year's resolution strategy in a survey conducted in January 2023. Lavars was also interviewed in March 2023.

30 **Miracle Question:** The Miracle Question and the story of Felix and Elaine come from Metcalf, L. (2004). *The Miracle Question: Answer It and Change Your Life*. Norwalk, CT: Crown House Publishing.

33 **VA loan forgiveness:** The VA loans story is drawn from interviews with two Department of Education officials conducted separately from March 2022 to April 2024; both asked to remain anonymous because they were not authorized to speak publicly. Also interviewed were Alex Edson from the National Student Legal Defense Network and Walter Ochinko from Veterans Education Success, in April 2024. Additional sources include: Patrick Campbell and Brian Lavin's

"Check your mailbox: Veterans with severe disabilities and student loans should keep an eye out for this," Consumer Financial Protection Bureau, July 19, 2018, https://www.consumerfinance.gov/about-us /blog/check-your-mailbox-veterans-severe-disabilities-and-student -loans-should-keep-eye-out/; Patrick Campbell and Seth Frotman's "Help is here for people with severe disabilities struggling with student loans," Consumer Financial Protection Bureau, February 7, 2018 https://www.consumerfinance.gov/about-us/blog/help-here-people -severe-disabilities-struggling-student-loans/; the Petition to Amend Regulations Before the US Department of Education, filed by the National Student Legal Defense Network, Community Legal Aid Society Inc. of Delaware, and Justice in Aging, April 19, 2021, https:// www.defendstudents.org/news/body/2021.04.19-Final-Petition-re -TPD-Rulemaking3.pdf; and Federal Student Aid's Automatic Total and Permanent Disability Discharge through Social Security Administration Data Match, August 19, 2021, https://fsapartners.ed.gov /knowledge-center/library/electronic-announcements/2021-08-19 /automatic-total-and-permanent-disability-discharge-through-so cial-security-administration-data-match-ea-id-general-21-49. The quote from the disabled veteran who had student loans forgiven is from Allison Norlian's "A Disabled Veteran Had Over $72,000 In Student Loans—Under The Biden Administration, Her Debt Was Forgiven," Forbes.com, September 20, 2021, https://www.forbes .com/sites/allisonnorlian/2021/09/20/a-disabled-veteran-had-over -72000-in-student-loans-under-the-biden-administration-her-debt -was-forgiven/.

CHAPTER 3 (STUDY THE BRIGHT SPOTS)

41 **Cockpit redesign:** The air force "average pilot" story is drawn from Todd Rose's book: Rose, T. (2016). *The End of Average: How We Succeed in a World That Values Sameness.* New York: HarperCollins.

44 **Ken Davis at Gartner:** Ken Davis's "bright spots" work with Gartner is drawn from interviews and email correspondence with Davis between February 2022 and April 2024.

55 **Million Cat Challenge:** The story of Kate Hurley's work with the Jacksonville shelter and the Million Cat Challenge comes from an interview in February 2024 and from Julie Castle's blog post "The Remarkable Dr. Kate Hurley: Evolution of a Cat Lifesaving Legend,"

Best Friends, November 7, 2018, https://bestfriends.org/stories/julie-castle-blog/remarkable-dr-kate-hurley-evolution-cat-lifesaving-legend. Information on shelter medicine is drawn from https://www.aspcapro.org/about-programs-services/shelter-medicine-and-aspca and University of California, Davis's resource https://www.sheltermedicine.com/. The conditions at the Jacksonville shelter and efforts to bring down its euthanasia rate are from an interview with Ebenezer Gujjarlapudi in March 2024. The San Jose, California, shelter's results with return to field are described in Johnson, K. L., & Cicirelli, J. (2014). Study of the effect on shelter cat intakes and euthanasia from a shelter neuter return project of 10,080 cats from March 2010 to June 2014. *PeerJ* 2, e646. Sources for the history of the Million Cat Challenge include Hurley's appearance on the *Unleashing Social Change* podcast, September 3, 2019, and Mary-Jo Dione's "Million Cat Challenge," *Best Friends* magazine, May/June 2015, http://digitaleditions.walsworthprintgroup.com/publication/index.php?i=252803&m=&l=&p=32&pre=&ver=html5#{%22page%22:34,%22issue_id%22:252803. Information on the Million Cat Challenge's five initiatives and managed admissions was found on the organization's website, specifically: https://www.millioncatchallenge.org/about/the-five-key-initiatives, https://www.millioncatchallenge.org/resources/managed-admission, and https://www.millioncatchallenge.org/about/faqs/lists/frequently-asked-questions/.

CHAPTER 4 (TARGET THE CONSTRAINT)

61   **The Chick-fil-A drive-thru:** This story was drawn from Dan's fateful Roxboro Road Chick-fil-A run and subsequent interview with Tony Fernandez in August of 2021, along with multiple check-ins with both Fernandez and colleague Jacob Franks since then. Drive-thru stats were drawn from "The 2023 QSR® Drive-Thru Report," *QSR*, September 28, 2023, https://www.qsrmagazine.com/reports/the-2023-qsr-drive-thru-report/.

68   **Norwood home health care:** This story is drawn from two interviews with Laura Shaw-deBruin in March 2023 and February 2024, as well as from Shaw-deBruin's interview with Miriam Allred on *The Care Leaders' Podcast* from September 2021: https://www.homecarepulse.com/podcast/launching-a-caregiver-mentorship-program/. General information about the home-care industry is from the "2021

Home Care Benchmarking Study," *Home Care Pulse*, 2021, https://www.homecarepulse.com/benchmarking/2021-study/.

72   **Sticky-note appreciations:** Laura Heck shared the story about "sticky-note appreciations" on Dan's podcast, *What It's Like to Be . . .* , in October 2023: https://www.whatitslitobe.com/2246914/13766525-a-couples-therapist.

CHAPTER 5 (MAP THE SYSTEM)

79   **Bursts:** Geordie Brackin and Mike Goldstein's high-dosage career counseling is drawn from an interview with Brackin in December 2022 and two interviews with Mike Goldstein in November 2022 and June 2023, plus multiple email exchanges, as well as their 1Up Career Coaching white paper: Bracklin, G., & Goldstein, M. (June 2023). *Peeling the "College Career Services Office" Onion*, https://tinyurl.com/peelingcareeronion, and the report where they compiled the results for their first cohort in 2021. Faith Carter was interviewed in January 2023 and Michael Deleon in December 2022. The Bain study of charter school graduates was called the "Alumni Success Project," commissioned by the Charter School Growth Fund in February 2020.

86   **UIHC radiology department:** The UIHC's breakthrough kaizen sprint is recounted in Bahensky, J. A., Roe, J., & Bolton, R. (2005). "Lean sigma—will it work for healthcare?" *Journal of Healthcare Information Management* 19(1), 39–44, https://www.researchgate.net/publication/8049032_Lean_sigma--will_it_work_for_healthcare. James Bahensky was interviewed in May 2023 and Romy Bolton in April 2023.

89   **Methane and the EDF:** The EDF's approach to tracking methane emissions is drawn from an interview with Steven Hamburg in February 2024. Southwestern Energy's Mark Boling was interviewed in February 2024. The MethaneSAT project was announced by EDF's Fred Krupp in a 2018 TED Talk, https://www.youtube.com/watch?v=5qzy1fHYQNg. Sources for additional information include Jonathan Mingle's "The Methane Detectives: On the Trail of a Global Warming Mystery," *Undark*, May 13, 2019, https://undark.org/2019/05/13/methane-global-warming-climate-change-mystery/, Alejandra Borunda's "Methane, explained," *National Geographic*, January 23, 2019, https://www.nationalgeographic.com/environment/article/methane, and a 2021 TED Talk by the EDF's Illisa Ocko,

https://www.ted.com/talks/ilissa_ocko_the_fastest_way_to_slow_cli
mate_change_now.

CHAPTER 6 (START WITH A BURST)

101 **Home Depot:** The Home Depot hose system saga was shared in a
blog post by Greg McLawsen, "How lawyers can use Agile project
management and kanban," Sound Immigration, April 28, 2016, https://
www.soundimmigration.com/agile/.

105 **Time confetti:** Brigid Schulte shares the personal consequences of
her fragmented free time in her book: Schulte, B. (2014). *Overwhelmed:
Work, Love, and Play When No One Has the Time*. New York: Sarah
Crichton Books. Ashley Whillans writes about time confetti and its
effect on happiness in her book: Whillans, A. (2020). *Time Smart: How
to Reclaim Your Time and Live a Happier Life*. Brighton, MA: Harvard
Business Review Press. An excerpt from *Time Smart* about identifying and overcoming time confetti was published in *Behavioral Scientist*:
"Time Confetti and the Broken Promise of Leisure," *Behavioral Scientist*, October 7, 2020, https://behavioralscientist.org/time-confetti
-and-the-broken-promise-of-leisure/.

106 **Design sprints:** Jake Knapp, John Zeratsky, and Braden Kowitz's
book introduces the design sprint methodology: Knapp, J., Zeratsky,
J., & Kowitz, B. (2016). *Sprint: How to Solve Big Problems and Test New
Ideas in Just Five Days*. New York: Simon & Schuster.

107 **The many meanings of silence:** The teams who struggled to interpret the meaning of each other's silence were a part of Catherine Durnell Cramton's 2001 study on dispersed teams: Durnell, C. D. (2001).
"The mutual knowledge problem and its consequences for dispersed
collaboration." *Organization Science* 12(3), 346–71.

108 **Bursty communication:** The idea of bursty communication is drawn
from Christoph Riedl and Anita Williams Woolley, "'Bursty' Communication Can Help Remote Teams Thrive," *Behavioral Scientist*,
May 29, 2018, https://behavioralscientist.org/bursty-communication
-can-help-remote-teams-thrive/. The original study featured in the
piece is here: Riedl, C., & Woolley, A. W. (2016). "Teams vs. Crowds:
A Field Test of the Relative Contribution of Incentives, Member Ability, and Emergent Collaboration to Crowd-Based Problem Solving
Performance." *Academy of Management Discoveries* 3(4), 382–403.

109 **Technical Data Center turnaround:** The turnaround at ExxonMobil's

Technical Data Center was drawn from two interviews with Matthew Knies in January and April of 2024 and a supporting interview with one of his colleagues in April 2024.

112 **The middle problem of motivation:** Ayelet Fishbach recommends shortening the middle in her book: Fishbach, A. (2022). *Get It Done: Surprising Lessons from the Science of Motivation*. New York: Little, Brown Spark. The "look backward, then look forward" strategy comes from an article by Peter Gwynne, "Mastering Motivation," *Kellogg Insight*, August 3, 2012, https://insight.kellogg.northwestern.edu /article/mastering_motivation. The article features original research by Andrea Bonezzi, Miguel Brendl, and Matteo De Angelis: Bonezzi, A. C., Brendl, M., & De Angelis, M. (2011). "Stuck in the Middle: The Psychophysics of Goal Pursuit." *Psychological Science* 22(5), 607–12.

CHAPTER 7 (RECYCLE WASTE)

119 **Asheboro trash trucks:** The story of how the City of Asheboro figured out how to cut waste from their bulk trash pickups came from a case study by city manager John Ogburn, compiled for the International City/County Management Association (ICMA). Additional details came from a report: "City of Asheboro, NC, Reduces Expenses and Improves Efficiency with Mobile311™," *Dude Solutions*, https:// www.brightlysoftware.com/sites/default/files/2020-09/asheboro-case study.pdf.

120 **DOWNTIME:** A DOWNTIME analysis of the receiving area situation at Northwestern can be found in the 2019 case study and accompanying teaching note by John P. McNicholas, Hussam Bachour, and Paul Suett: Nicholas, J., Bachour, H., & Suett, P. (2019). "Northwestern Memorial Hospital: Smoothing Material Flow Through the Receiving Area." Ivey Publishing.

122 **Sweetgreen's new bowls:** The original Sweetgreen story came from Christian Paz, "Here's Why Sweetgreen Is Switching to Hexagonal Bowls," *Washingtonian*, August 17, 2018, https://www.washingtonian .com/2018/08/17/heres-why-sweetgreen-is-switching-to-hexagonal -bowls/. More details came from an interview with Sweetgreen CEO Jonathan Neman in January 2019.

125 **A seamless church service:** The no-waste worship story came from an interview with Graham Standish in September 2023 and email communication in 2024.

127   **Shifting right:** The story of shifting right to free up underwriter time came from an interview with Gary Kaplan in April 2023 and an interview with Gary Kaplan and David Grigg in May 2023.

129   **The Pixar pivot:** Ed Catmull tells the story of his decision to eliminate the Pixar oversight group to protect the creative team in his book: Catmull, E., & Wallace, A. (2023). *Creativity, Inc. (The Expanded Edition)*. New York: Random House.

130   **Eighteen hours of sales forecasting:** The story of the VP who spends 18 hours on forecasting calls every week was shared in an interview with an account executive at a software company in January 2024 who wanted to remain anonymous for obvious reasons.

130   **Type 1 versus Type 2 decisions:** Jeff Bezos wrote about Type 1 versus Type 2 decisions in his 1997 letter to Amazon shareholders: https://www.sec.gov/Archives/edgar/data/1018724/000119312516530910/d168744dex991.htm.

CHAPTER 8 (DO LESS AND MORE)

137   **Rosa and her seven-year-old daughter:** Rosa's story comes from John J. Murphy's book: Murphy, J. J. (2023). *Solution-Focused Therapy*. Washington, DC: American Psychological Association.

140   **The 80/20 rule at Strategex:** Interviews with David Philippi in February 2023 and April 2024. For more on using the 80/20 principle in business, see also this blog post by Barry Holt, "Understanding the 80/20 Principle," Strategex, July 28, 2021, https://strategex.com/insights/understanding-the-80-20-principle, and this presentation by Mark Fooksman from January 13, 2022: https://www.youtube.com/watch?v=7Xumo2HULBw.

145   **STOP, START, LESS, MORE:** The four-quadrant exercise came from Ari Medoff (via a conversation in September 2023) and his colleague Jennifer Axelson.

146   **Big Brothers Big Sisters:** The story of the Big Brothers Big Sisters turnaround is drawn from interviews with Art Mollenhauer in February 2023 and March 2024. See also the 2016 report by Donald Haider, Katherine Cooper, and Reyhaneh Maktoufi, "Mergers as a Strategy for Success: 2016 Report from the Metropolitan Chicago Nonprofit Merger Research Project," Mission Plus Strategy Consulting and Chicago Foundation for Women, 2016, https://chicagonpmergerstudy.org/.

150   **"You cannot save your way to health:"** This quote comes from

Michael Kaiser's book: Kaiser, M. M. (2008). *The Art of the Turnaround: Creating and Maintaining Healthy Arts Organizations*. Waltham, MA: Brandeis University Press.

150 **Companies post-recession:** The companies who did less and more to weather a recession were part of research by Ranjay Gulati, Nitin Nohria, and Franz Wohlgezogen, "Roaring Out of Recession," *Harvard Business Review*, March 2010, https://hbr.org/2010/03/roaring -out-of-recession.

CHAPTER 9 (TAP MOTIVATION)

157 **Ezra Fox was struggling to get his kids to clean up their room:** From an interview with Ezra Fox in October 2023 and subsequent email correspondence.

158 **Dr. Doug Eby:** Information on Southcentral and the Nuka System of Care is drawn from an interview with Dr. Eby in March 2022, his keynote presentation at a 2010 Canadian Health Services Research Foundation conference (in two parts: https://www.youtube .com/watch?v=tLnZ3_AccoU and https://www.youtube.com/watch ?v=5TfNjYshPsc), the Southcentral Foundation's website, https://www .southcentralfoundation.com/, and the Nuka System of Care website, https://scfnuka.com/.

159 **John J. Murphy:** The quote is from an interview with Murphy in September 2023.

163 **"Genius swap":** The genius swap inspiration comes from multiple chats with Becky Margiotta over the years and follow-up email correspondence in 2023.

164 **Dianne Connery and the library in Pottsboro, Texas:** Information on a dramatic turnaround at the Pottsboro Library is drawn from two interviews with Connery in December 2022 and January 2023 and email correspondence in June 2023 and December 2023; Connery's 2016 talk, "Flip The Script: Changing the Direction of the Library," from the Nebraska Library Commission's *Big Talk from Small Libraries* series, https://www.youtube.com/watch?v=hxAzYqWtqMU; as well as the following sources: ITDRC, "More Than Books—The Pottsboro Library is a Guiding Light for the Community," Medium, December 14, 2020, https://medium.com/@ITDRC/more-than-books-the-pottsboro -library-is-a-guiding-light-for-the-community-853c6178193d, "Dianne Connery: Movers & Shakers 2021," *Library Journal*, June 8, 2021,

https://www.libraryjournal.com/story/dianne-connery-movers-shakers
-2021%E2%80%93innovators, Ali Montag, "Beyond Books in Pottsboro," *Texas Observer*, November 30, 2021, https://www.texasobserver
.org/beyond-books-in-pottsboro/, and Lauren Rangel, "Pottsboro
Library named finalist for highest national honor in libraries," *KXII*,
March 28, 2023, https://www.kxii.com/2023/03/28/pottsboro-library
-named-finalist-highest-national-honor-libraries/.

166   *Seinfeld* **episode:** Transcribed from *Seinfeld*, Season 5, Episode 22,
"The Opposite."

169   **Frank Blake, the former CEO of Home Depot:** Blake's approach
is drawn from an interview with him in January 2024 and from his
appearance on *The Tim Ferriss Show*, Episode #303, March 22, 2018,
https://tim.blog/2018/03/22/the-tim-ferriss-show-transcripts-frank
-blake/.

CHAPTER 10 (LET PEOPLE DRIVE)

179   **Self-dialysis:** The self-dialysis story comes from a number of sources,
including an interview with Richard Gibney in May 2023, Merry
Smith in May 2023, and Eugene Payne in April 2024. Richard Gibney writes about self-care dialysis in "From Sweden to Texas via the
IHI National Forum: Do-It-Yourself Dialysis," Institute for Healthcare Improvement, August 3, 2016, https://web.archive.org/web/202
30421105046/https:/www.ihi.org/communities/blogs/from-sweden
-to-texas-via-the-ihi-national-forum-do-it-yourself-dialysis, and "How
Can Self-Care Dialysis Improve Outcomes?" Empowered Kidney
Care, August 20, 2020, https://empoweredkidneycare.org/blog/how
-can-self-care-dialysis-improve-outcomes/. More information about
Empowered Kidney Care can be found on their website, https://
empoweredkidneycare.org/. Christian Farman's story is described in
the article "A Patient Directs His Own Care," Institute for Healthcare
Improvement, 2012, https://web.archive.org/web/20230926130301
/https:/www.ihi.org/resources/Pages/ImprovementStories/APatient
DirectsHisOwnCareFarmanSelfDialysis.aspx.

182   **Archery coach Guy Krueger:** The story of Guy Krueger comes from
interviews with him in September 2022 and March 2024.

183   **Gabriele Wulf and external focus of attention:** Gabriele Wulf's work
on external focus of attention and coaching comes from an interview
with her in August 2024 and her article: Wulf, G., & Lewthwaite, R.

(2021). "Translating Thoughts Into Action: Optimizing Motor Performance and Learning Through Brief Motivational and Attentional Influences." *Current Directions in Psychological Science* 30(6), 535–41.

187   **Jobs survey:** The information on what people want from their jobs comes from a reader survey Dan conducted in 2021.

187   **Spotify:** Details of Spotify's engineering culture comes from this 2019 video by Henrik Kniberg: https://www.youtube.com /watch?v=Yvfz4HGtoPc.

189   **"The opposite of trust . . .":** Ken Blanchard's quote is from Blanchard, K., & Conley, R. (2022). *Simple Truths of Leadership: 52 Ways to Be a Servant Leader and Build Trust.* Oakland, CA: Berrett-Koehler Publishers.

191   **T-Mobile:** The story of T-Mobile's customer service transformation comes from an interview with Jon Freier in July 2022 and with Lisa Jones in March 2024. Also the piece draws extensively from an article by Matthew Dixon, "Reinventing Customer Service," *Harvard Business Review*, November–December, 2018, https://hbr.org/2018/11 /reinventing-customer-service.

CHAPTER 11 (ACCELERATE LEARNING)

201   **San Francisco 49ers:** Interview with Moon Javaid in March 2024. The following sources served as background for Javaid's efforts to get better, faster feedback: Javaid's presentation at the Sports Innovation Summit in 2018, https://www.youtube.com/watch?v=QzAMEGPIC8w, and David Owen's "Customer Satisfaction at the Push of a Button," *The New Yorker*, February 5, 2018, https://www.newyorker.com/mag azine/2018/02/05/customer-satisfaction-at-the-push-of-a-button, as well as Javaid's podcast appearances on *Sports Innovation Lab*, December 7, 2021, https://www.sportsilab.com/podcast/moonjavaidpodcast, *Stadium Tech Report*, June 2, 2022, https://www.stadiumtechreport .com/podcasts/we-talk-stadium-concessions-innovation-with-49ers -cso-moon-javaid/, and *Flip the Switch*, May 29, 2020, https://en gagemintpartners.com/measuring-customer-experience/. The warm stadium-wine incident is from Jabari Young's "San Francisco 49ers removing game-day barriers in real time with its SAP data war room," CNBC, December 24, 2019, https://www.cnbc.com/2019/12/24 /san-francisco-49ers-removing-game-day-barriers-with-sap-software .html.

207   **Tom Chi/Schmidt:** Tom [...] back is drawn from an intervie[...] to soliciting actionable feed- Effective Session Outcomes" at G[...] 2024 and his talk "Getting .youtube.com/watch?v=z_elgzL9sns. [...]n in 2018, https://www

212   **Scrum:** The analysis of agile and the water[...] an interview with J. J. Sutherland in January 202[...]hodology is from Sutherland, J., & Sutherland, J. J. (2014). *Scrum: The* [...]e book *Scrum*: *the Work in Half the Time*. New York: Crown Currency. *Doing Twice*

212   **NPR:** The story behind NPR's agile-inspired productions [...] from interviews with Eric Nuzum in October 2023 and March 2[...], as well as Andrew Phelps's article "Agile, social, cheap: The new way NPR is trying to make radio," Nieman Journalism Lab, April 27, 2012, https://www.niemanlab.org/2012/04/agile-social-cheap-the-new-way -npr-is-trying-to-make-radio/.

CONCLUSION

219   **Hospital Sírio-Libanês:** The Joy at Work intervention at Hospital Sírio-Libanês comes from interviews with Wania Regina Mollo Baia in January and February 2023 and a number of materials shared by her; an interview with Jessica Perlo in November 2021; and interviews with Natália Paranhos de Araújo and Nilda Rosa de Oliveira Prado in January 2023. The IHI Framework for Improving Joy in Work can be found at https://www.ihi.org/resources/white-papers/ihi-framework -improving-joy-work.

Index

About the Author

DAN HEATH is the #1 *New York Times* bestselling coauthor/author of six books, including *Made to Stick*, *Switch* and *The Power of Moments*. His books have sold more than four million copies worldwide and have been translated into thirty-five languages. Dan also hosts the award-winning podcast *What It's Like to Be . . .*, which explores what it's like to walk in the shoes of people from different professions (a mystery novelist, a cattle rancher, a forensic accountant, and more). A graduate of the University of Texas at Austin and Harvard Business School, he lives in Durham, North Carolina.